"In this book, Jerry challenges [...] addressing outward behavior. [...] gospel is one that teenagers will be able to grasp and apply to their lives. This book needs to be a part of every youth curriculum."

—TYLER CLEMENTS, director of Youth Ministries, Grace EPC, Lawrence, Kansas

"In all of Jerry's writings and speaking, he invites us to something, someone, much greater and more beautiful. His passion for the gospel has forever changed my life. He reminds us that a correct appropriation of the gospel should always lead to a greater hunger for holiness, never apathy. It is the gospel that gives us hope to not live in the shame of the sins we struggle with as we continue on this journey toward more of Jesus in our lives."

—MARK MCELMURRY, associate dean of students, Covenant Theological Seminary

"Simple. Clear. Rich. Gospel-centered. Everything you would expect from Jerry Bridges. For teens to have these categories of sin in their minds, experience the life-transforming power of the gospel, and know how to handle these issues biblically are gifts that will bless them for the rest of their lives. I'm jealous for our youth to benefit from this book."

—MICHAEL PLEWNIAK, pastor, Cornerstone Church of Knoxville

"Anyone serious about discipling teens must traverse the rocky terrain of their sin along the beautiful landscape of the gospel. Jerry Bridges here brings the 'boring' sins of everyday Christianity under the blinding light and magnifying glass of God's holiness. I have been utterly humbled as the wonder of my Father's love has been revealed in contrast to my respectable sins."

—REV. DREW T. LINTS, pastor of students and families, Village Seven Presbyterian Church

# RESPECTABLE SINS

THE TRUTH ABOUT ANGER, JEALOUSY, WORRY,
AND OTHER STUFF WE ACCEPT

# JERRY BRIDGES

✳ STUDENT EDITION ✳

TH1NK, an
Imprint of
NavPress

**NAVPRESS**
Discipleship Inside Out®

NavPress is the publishing ministry of The Navigators, an international Christian organization and leader in personal spiritual development. NavPress is committed to helping people grow spiritually and enjoy lives of meaning and hope through personal and group resources that are biblically rooted, culturally relevant, and highly practical.

**For a free catalog go to www.NavPress.com**
**or call 1.800.366.7788 in the United States or 1.800.839.4769 in Canada.**

ISBN-13: 978-1-61291-496-1

Cover design by Studiogearbox

Adapted by Anne Christian Buchanan

Some of the anecdotal illustrations in this book are true to life and are included with the permission of the persons involved. All other illustrations are composites of real situations, and any resemblance to people living or dead is coincidental.

Unless otherwise identified, all Scripture quotations in this publication are taken from the Holy Bible, English Standard Version® (ESV®), copyright © 2001 by Crossway, a publishing ministry of Good News Publishers. ESV® Text Edition: 2011. Used by permission. All rights reserved; Other versions used include: the *Holy Bible, New International Version*® (NIV®). Copyright © 1973, 1978, 1984, 2011 by Biblica, Inc.™ Used by permission of Zondervan. All rights reserved worldwide. www.zondervan.com. The "NIV" and "New International Version" are trademarks registered in the United States Patent and Trademark Office by Biblica, Inc.®; *The New Testament in Modern English* (PH), J. B. Phillips Translator, © J. B. Phillips 1958, 1960, 1972, used by permission of Macmillan Publishing Company; and the King James Version (KJV).

Bridges, Jerry.
  Respectable sins : the truth about anger, jealousy, worry, and other stuff we accept / Jerry Bridges. -- Student Edition.
    pages cm
  Includes bibliographical references.
  ISBN 978-1-61291-496-1
  1. Sin--Christianity--Textbooks. I. Title.
  BT715.B75 2013
  241'.3--dc23
                        2013027027

Printed in the United States of America

1 2 3 4 5 6 7 8 / 18 17 16 15 14 13

# CONTENTS

# RESPECTABLE SIN?

If you've spent any time at all around churches, you know what sin is. It's the bad stuff. The wrong actions and attitudes that go against God.

Murder is a sin, right? Lying and cheating are sins. Sleeping around is sin. So is being greedy and exploiting people and ignoring the poor.

Most Christians I know would agree on those. So would many non-Christians.

But what about sin that isn't so obvious? What about the sin that we downplay or excuse or don't even notice in our lives?

That's what I call respectable sin, and it's what this book is all about.

You could also call it sneaky sin or subtle sin, or even "good Christian sin," because it's the kind that trips up good, respectable, Bible-reading people. People who grew up in church and gave their lives to Christ. People in Sunday school and youth group.

People like you, maybe.

Definitely people like me.

Most believers I know would never dream of murdering someone or robbing a bank. But what about talking about someone behind his back? Or thinking we're better than someone else? Or getting annoyed and lashing out sarcastically? Or being jealous when someone else gets something we want? (For a checklist of common respectable sins, turn to pages 52–53.)

Those are sins too, even if they don't seem as bad as the "biggies" like robbery or murder. And they're the sins that many good Christians minimize. Some of us even get so worked up about other people's "bad" sin or the sinful society "out there" that we completely overlook the sin in our own lives. That makes us hypocrites as well as sinners. It also can keep us stuck in our sin, because we've got to get real about sin before we can break free from it.

The good news of the gospel is that in the end God wins and sin loses. But we still need to take sin seriously—even the sneaky, respectable kind of sin.

That's why I wrote this book. I hope it helps you.

More importantly, I hope it inspires you to keep on turning to the One who is the answer to all our sin.

To Him be all the glory.

## PART ONE

# SAINTS AND SINNERS

# CHAPTER 1

# ME — A SAINT?

The church in the Roman town of Corinth was messed up. *Really* messed up. They were always squabbling among themselves and breaking up into cliques. They got drunk at the Lord's Supper. They tolerated all kinds of sexual immorality, even a man sleeping with his stepmother. They sued each other in court, abused their freedom in Christ, totally disrupted their own worship services, and got hopelessly confused about key elements of their faith.

And do you know what Paul called the Corinthian Christians?

He called them saints.

He addressed his first letter "to the church of God that is in Corinth, to those sanctified in Christ Jesus, called to be saints together with all those who in every place call upon the name of our Lord Jesus Christ" (1 Corinthians 1:2).

Today we wouldn't call those messed-up Corinthians saints. That's the name we use for really holy people, like the original apostles or other long-dead people who led spiritually outstanding lives. Or sometimes we'll refer to an unusually wise, godly person as a saint: "If there ever was a saint, it is my grandmother."

But the Corinthians weren't spiritually outstanding or especially godly. So why did Paul address them as saints?

Actually, Paul used that word other places too, and he always applied it to *ordinary believers* (see, for example, Romans 1:7; 16:15; 2 Corinthians 1:1; Ephesians 1:1; Philippians 1:1; 4:21-22; Colossians 1:2). That makes a little more sense when you look at what the Bible words really mean.

The Greek word for saint, *hagios*, means "one who is separated or set apart." It's related to *hagiadzo*, or "sanctified," which means "set aside for a special purpose, cleansed and holy." And *both* of those words show up in 1 Corinthians 1:2. It sounds a little awkward, but we could translate Paul's words as "to those separated in Christ Jesus, called to be separated ones."

Separated for what? A better question is, *Separated for whom?* And the answer is, "for God." Every true believer has been separated or set apart by God for God.

Read that again. Separated. Set apart. By God. For God.

If you're a believer, that means you!

*You* are a saint.

Titus 2:14 describes Jesus as the one "who gave himself for us to redeem us from all lawlessness and to purify for himself a people for his own possession." And 1 Corinthians 6:19-20 tells us, "You are not your own, for you were bought with a price." Together, these two passages help us understand the biblical meaning of a saint. It is someone Jesus bought with His own blood on the cross, someone set aside to belong to Him.

What does it mean to be set apart? To me, it's a little like what happens to the cadets who enter the U.S. Air Force Academy near our home. It's not your typical freshman experience! From the time they get off the bus at the Academy grounds, cadets undergo intense discipline—physical, mental, and emotional. The pressure eases up some over time, but it's never completely removed. Even seniors face heavy academic and behavioral demands.

Why are these cadets treated like this? Because the Academy doesn't exist to prepare schoolteachers or Wall Street bankers. It exists for one purpose: to prepare officers for the U.S. Air Force. The cadets are "set apart" for that purpose.

In a similar way, every new believer has been set apart by God for a purpose: to be transformed into the likeness of His Son, Jesus Christ. So in that sense, all believers are saints—separated from their old, sinful way of life and set apart to increasingly glorify God as their lives are transformed.

We don't become saints by our actions. We are *made* saints by the immediate supernatural action of the Holy Spirit, who works this change deep within our inner being. In fact, we actually become new creations in Christ (see 2 Corinthians 5:17). We've been "delivered . . . from the domain of darkness and transferred . . . to the kingdom of his beloved Son" (Colossians 1:13).

This change of state is described prophetically in Ezekiel 36:26: "I will give you a new heart and put a new spirit in you; I will remove from you your heart of stone and give you a heart of flesh" (NIV). Quite a transformation—from dead, unresponsive hearts to living, responsive ones. And that's what happens in us when we become believers.

But here's where it gets tricky, because even after we are made saints, we keep on sinning. Sad but true. We do it all the time—nearly every waking hour, in thought, word, or deed. Even if we do something good, our motives are often impure or mixed. The messed-up Corinthian church stands as Exhibit A for the reality that saints can be *very* sinful in our attitudes and actions.

Why the disconnect between what God has seemingly promised—a whole new, set-apart life—and what we experience in our daily lives? It's because there's something inside of us that fights against the new person we've become. As 1 Peter 2:11 puts it, the "passions of the flesh . . . wage war against your soul." Even though a decisive change always occurs in the heart of every new believer, that change doesn't immediately show itself in that person's attitudes and actions. It takes time and struggle, and the war is never completely over in this life. (We'll talk more about this battle in chapter 4.)

But that doesn't mean we have an excuse for sinful behavior! The whole point of the battle is to move toward becoming what we already are, what Jesus has already made us: His saints. That's why Paul began his first letter to the Corinthian church by reminding them that they were "sanctified in Christ Jesus, called to be saints." Then he spent the remainder of his letter vigorously urging them to live up to that calling.

He was saying, "You are saints. Now act like saints!"

Or as it's sometimes put, "Be what you are."

When I served in the U.S. Navy many years ago, there was an expression, "conduct unbecoming an officer." It covered anything from minor offenses to major ones that required a court martial. But the expression was more than a description of wrong behavior. It was a statement of what was *expected* of us as officers. Someone accused of "conduct unbecoming" had failed to live up to his responsibility to act as an officer should act.

Perhaps we need a similar expression for believers: "conduct unbecoming a saint." But wait! We do have a word for that: *sin*. And just as "conduct unbecoming an officer" covers a wide range of misconduct, the word *sin* covers a wide range of misbehavior, from gossip to adultery, from impatience to murder. Obviously, there are degrees of seriousness. But in the final analysis, sin is sin. It is conduct unbecoming a saint.

All believers, in other words, are like the Corinthians. We are saints, set aside by God for God, who more often than not don't act like saints.

Which is another way of saying that all of us saints are sinners. And it's time to take both our sainthood and our sneaky sins a little more seriously.

## YOUR TURN

"To those <u>sanctified</u> in Christ Jesus, <u>called</u> to be saints together with all those who in every place <u>call upon the name of our Lord Jesus Christ</u>.... <u>Grace</u> to you and <u>peace</u> from God our Father and the Lord Jesus Christ." (1 Corinthians 1:2-3)

## ENGAGE

1. How have you heard the word *saint* used in your experience? What does it feel like to be called a saint? I've always though a saint was when near perfection was reached. It feels awesome! I've never been called one before – certainly never thought I would.

2. Read 1 Peter 2:9-11. What do these verses tell you about being "set apart by Christ for Christ"? We were set apart by Christ for Christ to proclaim His name and proclaim His praises.

3. Name a time when the "war against your soul" felt especially real to you. How did that situation resolve itself? When hatred kept building and building inside of me for another human being. The Holy Spirit showed me through the Word that my hatred needed to be delt with. He helped me confess it (recognize it) and stop my hatred.

## BRING IT TO GOD

Take a minute to meditate on what it means to be a saint—what an incredible privilege and responsibility. Then thank God for saving you and ask Him to help you act like what you already are.

Saint: set apart for a special purpose; cleansed and holy.

# CHAPTER 2

# ME — A SINNER?

People used to hear about sin a lot more than they do now. In fact, when was the last time you heard the word *sin* used anywhere besides church?

C. S. Lewis noticed this when he was writing books like the Chronicles of Narnia series and *The Screwtape Letters*: "The barrier I have met is the total absence from the minds of my audience of any sense of sin."[1]

Famous psychiatrist Karl Menninger noticed it too back in 1979: "The very word, 'sin' . . . was once a strong word, an ominous and serious word. . . . [It] has almost disappeared—the word, along with the notion. Why? Doesn't anyone sin anymore? Doesn't anyone believe in sin?"[2]

More recently, in 2001 New Testament scholar D. A. Carson commented that the most frustrating aspect of doing evangelism in universities was the fact that students generally have no idea of sin. "They know *how to sin* well enough, but they have no idea of what constitutes sin."[3]

The whole idea of sin has pretty much disappeared from our culture and even from many of our churches. If it's there, it's been softened for modern sensibilities. We rarely hear about actions being wrong or immoral. Instead, we hear that someone did something "inappropriate" or "made a mistake."

You might say, "But I hear about sin all the time at church!" And that may be true, especially if you go to a conservative evangelical church. But take a minute to think about *how* sin is talked about and how you usually think about it.

A youth leader invited a bunch of kids from his church to join him in prayer for their school and community. And every one of those kids talked about bad things they'd heard about in society or seen other kids do—stuff like drugs, sex, cheating, abortion. No one prayed about their own temptations or the struggles of people they hung out with. Finally the frustrated group leader closed the meeting with the story of the tax collector in one of Jesus' parables: "God, be merciful to me, a sinner!" (Luke 18:13).

I've seen that happen in a lot of churches and Christian organizations. We see sin so easily in the immoral or unethical conduct of people in society at large. But we often fail to see it in what I call the "acceptable sins of the saints"—those sneaky, respectable sins we talked about at the beginning of this book. So we end up living in denial: "We're not sinners. They are!"

Not all Christians do this, of course. But a lot of them do. They say snarky things about a brother or sister in Christ and feel just fine about it. They hold grudges over past wrongs without any effort to forgive as God has forgiven us. They look down their religious noses at sinners "out there" in the world without any sense of their own failures.

It's easy to let ourselves off the hook by saying that our "minor" sins are not as bad as the flagrant ones of society. But sin is sin, and God has not given us the authority to assign values for different sinful actions. In fact, He said through James, "Whoever keeps the whole law but fails *in one point* has become accountable for all of it" (2:10, italics mine).

Did you get that? If we fail to follow just one little bit of God's law, we're accountable for—that is, guilty of breaking—all of it!

If that's hard for you to wrap your mind around, it's because most of us tend to think in terms of individual laws and their penalties. But God's law is seamless. The Bible doesn't speak about God's *laws*, as in many of them; it speaks of God's *law*, as a single whole. A person who commits murder breaks God's law. So does a person who is jealous or anxious.

But aren't some sins more serious than others? Yes . . . and no. I would rather be angry at people or insult them than actually commit murder. Yet Jesus said all three actions will be judged (see Matthew 5:21-22). He also said that having sexual thoughts about someone we're not married to is as bad as having sex with that person (see verses 27-28).

The truth is, *all* sin is serious because all sin is a breaking of God's seamless law.

The apostle John put it this way: "Sin is lawlessness" (1 John 3:4). Whenever we sin, we're rejecting God's moral standards of right and wrong so that we can have our own way.

In Greek culture, *sin* originally meant to "miss the mark," that is, to miss the center of the target. Sin was considered a miscalculation or a failure to achieve. And there is some truth in that idea. Think of a person who feels really bad about some sinful behavior and keeps trying to change, only to fail again and again.

But let's be honest. Most of our sinful actions are not failed efforts to do the right thing. They're *successful* efforts to do exactly what we want. As James wrote, "Each person is tempted when he is lured and enticed by his own desire" (1:14). We sin because the pleasure or satisfaction of our sinful behavior is stronger than our desire to please God.

Sin is sin. Even the sin that doesn't seem so bad to us is serious in God's eyes. The apostle Paul quoted the Old Testament to remind us: "Cursed be everyone who does not abide by *all things* written in the Book of the Law, and do them" (Galatians 3:10, italics mine).

"All things" is a tough standard. In school terms, that means a 99 on a final exam is a failing grade. It means that one misplaced comma in an otherwise fine term paper would get you an F.

Paul did go on to assure us that Christ has "redeemed us from the curse of the law by becoming a curse for us" (verse 13). But that doesn't change the fact that even the "minor" sins we tolerate in our lives are completely "curseworthy."

The whole idea of sin may have almost disappeared from our culture. It may have been softened in many churches to save people from feeling uncomfortable. It might have been redefined by other Christians to cover only the big sins of society. But sin has not disappeared from the sight of God. All sins, both the respectable sins of the saints we too often tolerate and the flagrant sins of society we are quick to condemn, are terrible in God's sight. They *all* deserve His curse.

If this sounds harsh, let me hasten to stress that there are many godly, humble people who don't deny or excuse their respectable sins. But there are plenty who are quite judgmental toward the grosser sins of society and seem pridefully unaware of their own personal sins. A lot of us live somewhere in between. And all of us are lawless sinners deserving of God's judgment.

So . . . are you depressed yet? I promise you—there's hope!

God is still our heavenly Father, and He is at work among us to call us to repentance and renewal. But part of that work is to show us what we need to repent of—including those sneaky sins we tolerate in our own lives.

And so for one more chapter, we will dig deeper into the sinfulness of our respectable sins.

# YOUR TURN

"Sin is lawlessness." (1 John 3:4)

## ENGAGE

1. Do you agree that "the whole idea of sin has pretty much disappeared from our culture and even from many of our churches"? Why or why not? What have you heard about sin as you've grown up? *Yes, I think people are so blinded by having fun that they don't stop and think about what they're doing. Sin is what separates me from God. Sin is going against God.*

2. Make a list of attitudes and behavior you've noticed in yourself and others that might qualify as sneaky or respectable sins. Compare it to the list on pages 52–53. Anything you would change about either list? Any items hit especially close to home? *jealousy, lust, pride, weeds of anger.*

3. Read Matthew 7:1-5. How do these words of Jesus apply to the idea of respectable sin? Why do you think believers often focus on the sins of unbelievers rather than on their own personal sins? *I know I don't want to admit that I'm imperfect, and I try to say that I'm not as bad as THAT person!*

## BRING IT TO GOD

Ask God to forgive you for any times you've pointed out someone else's sin while overlooking your own. Pray for honesty, humility, and courage as you look your sneaky sins in the face and deal with them.

# CHAPTER 3

# SPIRITUAL CANCER

*ancer.* That word will stop you in your tracks, especially if you hear it applied to you or someone you love. That happened to me when my first wife was diagnosed with non-Hodgkin's lymphoma. I remember thinking, *This can't be happening to us.* But seventeen months later she was gone.

Cancer is a condition in which certain kinds of body cells start growing uncontrollably. Sometimes they invade the tissue around them. Sometimes they jump into the bloodstream or the lymph system and metastasize (spread) through the body. Left alone, they will usually cause death. It's a horrible reality.

And so is sin.

In fact, you can think of sin as spiritual cancer. If it isn't stopped, it can spread and contaminate every area of our lives. Seemingly small sins can lead to more serious ones—lustful thoughts to illicit sex, anger to murder. Sin can even "metastasize" into the lives of other believers, tempting them to sin as well.

Sin, you see, is more than wrong actions, unkind words, or even those bad thoughts we never express. It's a *thing* deep inside of us. I call it a principle. You can also think of it as an inner force or a tendency, even a chronic disease. Our sinful actions, words, and thoughts are simply symptoms or expressions of this sin thing, which Paul called the flesh. (Some Bible versions translate this as "sinful nature.")

Don't get confused and think "the flesh" just refers to bodies or sexuality. Biblically speaking, it's the term for our basic, selfish impulses and desires. It's such a powerful reality within us that Paul sometimes spoke of it as a living person (see Romans 7:8-11; Galatians 5:17). And it unfortunately sticks around after we become believers. Even though our hearts have been renewed, even though we are saints set apart for God's purposes, our flesh still fights for control.

If we fail to understand that, we make it easy for the sin in our lives to metastasize. Even our sneaky, respectable sin. Maybe *especially* that kind of sin, because we tend to ignore it.

The disease of cancer can be tricky, even deceitful. It can lurk unnoticed for years and reappear when you think you've beaten it. That's exactly the way respectable sin operates in our lives. Its effect on us is subtle and easily overlooked.

Subtle is the very opposite of obvious or in-your-face. That word can be used in a good sense to mean delicate or refined. But it can also mean wily, crafty, or treacherous—yes, sneaky. Subtle sins deceive us into thinking they are not so bad . . . or thinking they're not really sins . . . or not even thinking about them at all. It's easy to live in denial about this kind of sin or gloss over how bad it really is.

The seventeenth-century Puritan pastor Ralph Venning didn't do that. His book *The Sinfulness of Sin* describes sin as vile, ugly, odious, malignant, pestilent, pernicious, hideous, spiteful, poisonous, virulent, villainous, abominable, and deadly.[1] Sounds like he was describing a supervillain in a movie or graphic novel! In Venning's view, all our sin, even the sneaky, subtle stuff we might not consider sin, is supervillain bad. To tolerate it in our spiritual lives is as dangerous to us as tolerating cancer in our bodies.

But sin is not just harmful to us. It affects God, too.

I once heard someone describe sin as cosmic treason. That may sound over-the-top, especially when we're talking about "little" stuff like being sarcastic or holding a grudge. But think about it. God is absolutely pure, absolutely transcendent, the absolute Ruler over all creation. When we violate His law in any way, even with our "minor" sins, we're really rebelling against Him. Our sin really is cosmic treason. It's a rebellion and an affront. But it's something else as well—something more personal.

Do you know the story of David and Bathsheba? King David saw a beautiful woman and slept with her even though he knew she was married. Then he even arranged the death of her husband, Uriah, to cover up his adultery and married Bathsheba himself. To put it mildly, God was displeased with David's sin. He sent the prophet Nathan with a message for David: "Why have you *despised* the word of the LORD, to do what is evil in his sight? You have struck down Uriah . . . and have killed him with the sword of the Ammonites. Now therefore the sword shall never depart from your house, because you have *despised* me" (2 Samuel 12:9-10, italics mine).

Note the use of the word *despised* in this passage. First God accused David (through Nathan) of despising His Word. But then He said, "You have despised *me*." Don't get stuck on the awfulness of David's sin and miss the application of these words to our respectable sins. When we indulge in any sin, big or little, we are despising not only God's law, but God Himself. Think about that the next time you are tempted to blow off some "minor" sin!

But the bad news about our sin gets worse, because sin actually has the power to make God mourn. "Do not grieve the Holy Spirit of God," Paul wrote to the Ephesians, "by whom you were sealed for the day of redemption" (4:30). The apostle was warning the Ephesians about certain sins involving relationships—lying, stealing, lashing out in anger, tearing others down with our speech, treating others unkindly (see verses 25-32). And he implied that God actually experiences sadness when we do stuff like that because He's not just our Ruler and Judge, but also our loving Father and our Redeemer. He cares about what happens to us and how we treat each other, and our disobedience actually causes Him pain.

And don't let the sneaky nature of sin fool you into thinking that sin doesn't matter because God forgives it. God does forgive, but He never overlooks or tolerates sin. He *always* judges it. The difference for believers is that God has judged our sin in the person of His Son. Do we really want to presume on His grace and tolerate in ourselves the very sin that nailed Christ to the cross?

And don't forget that your every sinful thought and word and deed is done in the presence of God. Paul told us that God even understands our inner motives, that He "will disclose the purposes of the heart" (1 Corinthians 4:5). When we sin, it's like we're acting it out right before God's royal throne.

It doesn't matter whether our sin is scandalous or respectable. It's still sinful, only sinful, and altogether sinful, and it's heinous in the sight of God. God forgives our sin because of the shed blood of Christ, but He does not tolerate it. Instead, every sin that we commit, even the sin we don't even think about, was laid upon Christ as He bore the curse of God in our place.

Christ suffered because of our sin. That's the bad news about our sin, and, as you can see, it's really, really bad.

And how do you respond? Do you find yourself wishing that a certain other person would read this chapter? Or does this view of our sin make you want to fall on your knees before God and say you're sorry for all the sins you have tolerated in your life? Does it make you want to repent and find a way to live differently?

If the latter is true, then you are ready for the good news.

And it really is really, really good.

# YOUR TURN

"Do not grieve the Holy Spirit of God, by whom you were sealed for the day of redemption." (Ephesians 4:30)

## ENGAGE

1. This chapter compares sin to cancer and says it can "metastasize" in our lives and even into others' lives. Give an example of how you think this happens. *If I lie about something to get what I want, then my parents find out & are grieved. Then- it can have affect on my friends too if it involved them.*

2. What's Paul's term for the "sin thing" that lives deep inside us? In what specific ways do you feel its presence in your life? How do you usually try to fight it? *Our flesh. - Whenever I want a romantic entanglement. (In my head☺) I normally ask for God's strength because I can't fight it on my own.*

3. Why is it so important to take our "respectable sins" seriously? *Our respectable sins have the power to grieve our Heavenly Father just like any normal sin does. Jesus died for those too.*

## BRING IT TO GOD

Do what this chapter suggests. Actually get on your knees before God and say you're sorry for all the sins you have tolerated in your life. Ask for His forgiveness and His help in battling your sneaky sin.

# CHAPTER 4

# THE GUILT CURE

John Newton is famous for writing "Amazing Grace," the one hymn that everybody seems to know. But Newton didn't start out life as a hymn writer. In his youth, he was the captain of a slave ship! He left the sea and eventually became a Christian minister. But he never forgot the horrible nature of his sin as a slave trader. At the end of his life he told a friend, "My memory is nearly gone; but I remember two things: that I am a great sinner, and that Christ is a great Savior."[1]

Centuries before that, a man named Saul dedicated his life to persecuting Christians. He traveled from town to town to do it and even watched while a believer named Stephen was stoned to death. Then Saul met Jesus. He changed his name to Paul and spent the rest of his life preaching the gospel. But near the end of his ministry he wrote, "Christ Jesus came into the world to save sinners, of whom I am the foremost" (1 Timothy 1:15).

Do you think of yourself as a "great sinner"?

A lot of believers can't relate. They're not involved in slavery. They've never traveled from town to town to persecute people. They haven't murdered anyone or run a drug cartel or slept around. "No one's perfect," they might say, "but I'm not *that* bad."

If I look back on my own life, I have to admit I was generally a good kid. I got okay grades and didn't get in trouble much. I grew up to be a faithful husband and father and employee. I've even been on the staff of a Christian ministry for years and years.

And yet I've said hurtful, critical things to others. I've been resentful and impatient. I've acted selfishly, failed to trust God in difficult issues of life, succumbed to materialism. I've even let my favorite football team become an idol. And as we've seen, those sins are just as offensive to God as the more scandalous kind. So I have to agree with Paul that I am the foremost of sinners. Or with John Newton that "I am a great sinner" but "Christ is a great Savior."

That's my only hope, the only remedy for my cancerous sin.

It's your only remedy as well.

Note that Newton and Paul didn't say "I *was* a sinner." They said: "I *am*." This wasn't about slaves and persecution. They were painfully aware of still being sinners *right now*.

Paul, in fact, seems to have become more aware of his sinfulness as years went by. When he wrote to the Corinthians in AD 55, he referred to himself as "the least of the apostles" (1 Corinthians 15:9). Five years later, writing to the Ephesians, he called himself "the very least of all the saints" (3:8). And he called himself "the foremost of sinners" even later, in AD 63 or 64.

Was Paul getting more sinful as he went along? Of course not. Over the years, both Paul and John Newton acted more and more like the saints they had become at conversion. But they also became more aware of the sin that still remained in them.

John Newton could have easily said, "I *was* and *still am* a great sinner, but Christ is a great Savior." And if you and I are to make any progress in dealing with our sneaky sins, we must say the same. That's why we need the gospel every day of our lives.

A lot of Christians think that once we trust in Christ we don't need the gospel anymore, at least, not for ourselves; we just need to share it with unbelievers. But that's not true, as we've already seen. Though we truly are saints, we're practicing sinners too, and we need the gospel to keep that reality before us.

I'm using the word *gospel* here as a shorthand expression for what Jesus did through His historic life, death, and resurrection and what He is doing in our lives and our world through His Holy Spirit. This entire work of Christ is the remedy for the cancerous disease of sin. In fact, the great old hymn "Rock of Ages" calls it a "double cure":

- One, it takes care of guilt and makes us clean.
- And two, it frees us from sin's power.[2]

So how does the gospel of Jesus cleanse us of guilt? It starts by preparing our hearts to face the reality of our sin.

I'm not just talking a halfhearted admission that we've messed up! "Uh, sure, my bad, sorry about that." What's called for is a whole-hearted, defenseless facing of sin: "That was a really awful thing to do. I am a really selfish person, and that particular thing I did was only an outgrowth of the selfishness that still dwells within me. I really am a sinner."

But facing sin like that is painful. It makes us feel guilty. It should, because we *are* guilty. And if we believe, consciously or unconsciously, that God still counts our guilt against us, our sense of self-protection will kick in. We'll end up denying or at least minimizing our sin and guilt. Before we can even acknowledge our sin, let alone begin to deal with it, we need to know that God forgives us.

The gospel gives us that assurance: "Blessed are those whose lawless deeds are forgiven, and whose sins are covered; blessed is the man against whom the Lord will not count his sin" (Romans 4:7-8).

Why does God not count my sin against me? Because He has already charged it to Christ. As the prophet Isaiah wrote, "All we like sheep have gone astray; we have turned—every one—to his own way; and the Lord has *laid on him* the iniquity of us all" (53:6, italics mine).

The more deeply I can grasp this great truth of God's forgiveness of my sin through Christ, the more free I'll be to face my sin honestly and humbly. That's why it is so helpful to affirm each day with John Newton that "I am a great sinner, but Christ is a great Savior."

And here's another way the gospel cleanses us from guilt: It energizes and motivates us to deal with our sin. We are commanded in the

Bible to put sin to death (see Romans 8:13; Colossians 3:5). But some-times it's hard to find energy for what we're supposed to do. The gospel helps supply that energy in two ways. First, it *encourages* us that God is for us, not against us (see Romans 8:31). And that in turn *makes us grateful.* How can we not be thankful for what God has done and is now doing for us through Christ? This twofold effect of encourage-ment and gratitude together produces in us a *desire* to deal with our sin. It's what motivates us to deal with our respectable and subtle sins and act like the saints we already are.

You can see, then, that we need a daily dose of the gospel to deal with the sin in our lives. We need that daily assurance that even though we are great sinners, we have a great Savior. We need the continual reminder that our sins are forgiven, that God doesn't count them against us, that He is on our side and helping us fight against sin instead of judging us for it.

Some years ago, I heard a man use the expression, "Preach the gospel to yourself every day." That is what I believe we must do to deal with our sins, scandalous or respectable. We must remind ourselves of God's message of forgiveness and redemption and personalize it for ourselves, as Paul did when he wrote of "the Son of God, who loved *me* and gave himself for *me*" (Galatians 2:20, italics mine). There is never a day in our lives when we are so good that we don't need the gospel.

You may be wondering, *But how do I preach the gospel to myself anyway?* The whole idea might sound a little strange. So I'm going to tell you how I do it. Even if my way doesn't work for you, it might help you figure out your own way.

I begin each day by reminding myself that (1) I'm a saint and (2) I still sin every day in thought, word, deed, and motive. If I am aware of any recent sins in my life, big or little, I acknowledge those to God. Even if I can't think of any particular sins, I still acknowledge to God that I have not come close to loving Him with all my being or loving my neighbor as myself. That's always true, unfortunately!

Once my sins are out there, I repent of them. That is, I tell God I'm sorry and I want to change. Then I turn to specific Scriptures that assure me of God's forgiveness. Here are just a few I choose from each day: Psalm 103:12; 130:3-4; Isaiah 1:18; 38:17; 43:25; Micah 7:19; Romans 4:7-8; 8:1; 1 John 1:9.[3]

As I spend time with these Scriptures, I try to think about the way God's promise of forgiveness applies to my life. Sometimes I will paraphrase a Scripture to make it more personal. For instance, 1 John 4:10 will become: "This is love: not that *I* loved God, but that he loved *me* and sent his Son as an atoning sacrifice for *my* sins" (1 John 4:10, NIV—italics indicate personalized paraphrase).

Finally, I say to God—reminding myself!— that my only hope of a right standing with Him that day is Jesus' blood shed for my sins and His righteous life lived on my behalf.

That's the way I preach the gospel to myself. I hope you'll take this as a starting point and adapt it to your needs and personality. Maybe you'll want to write your sins and prayers in a notebook or sing a song that reminds you of the gospel message or use a Bible search engine to find Scriptures that apply to what you're seeing in your life. I predict that the more you do this, the closer you'll come to acting and feeling like the saint you are.

Being cleansed from guilt is a great thing. Understanding that God has forgiven all our sins through the death of His Son on the cross prepares us, frees us, and motivates us to face our ongoing sin.

But that's just the first half of the "double cure," remember. We'll look at the other half in the next chapter.

## YOUR TURN

"Blessed are those whose lawless deeds are forgiven, and whose sins are covered; blessed is the man against whom the Lord will not count his sin." (Romans 4:7-8)

### ENGAGE

1. This chapter says the gospel is a "double cure" for sin. What does this mean? *It does 2 things for us. There are 2 cures that are given.*

2. How does the truth that God has forgiven our sin free us to honestly and humbly face our sin? How does it motivate us to deal with our sin? *I can honestly + humbly face my sin because I know God loved me enough to put my sin on Christ. → I want to be more like Christ.*

3. What do you think of the idea of preaching the gospel to yourself every day? Would the author's plan for doing this work well for you? If not, what might? *It's awesome. Yes, I think it would work for me.*

4. The author lists Scriptures he uses to preach the gospel to himself. Choose one of these and write it down. What does it tell you about God's forgiveness? *Micah 7:19*

   *"He will again have compassion on us and subdue our iniquities. You will cast all our sins into the depths of the sea."*

   *His forgiveness isn't half-hearted. He goes so far as to cast our sin into the sea.*

## BRING IT TO GOD

Rework and personalize the Scripture you chose in number 4 and offer it to God as a prayer. (For instance, 1 John 4:10 could be "Dear God, thank You for loving me so much that You sent Your Son as an atoning sacrifice for my sins.")

Father in Heaven,

Thank you for having compassion on me and for subduing my iniquities. You didn't have to. Thank you for casting my sin into the depths of the sea.

# CHAPTER 5

# THE POWER CURE

Remember that double cure for sin that we talked about in the last chapter? Cleansing from guilt was the first part. The wonderful gospel truth that God forgives our sin through the death of His Son makes it possible to face the reality of our sin and actually begin fighting against it.

But guilt is only half the problem when it comes to sin. The other half involves the *power* sin has over us. Sometimes it feels like sin's in charge and we're helpless to resist. That's why we need the second half of the gospel's double cure—the power to break us free from sin's grip.

How does that work? It helps to think of the process as happening in two stages.

The first is our deliverance from the *rule* of sin in our lives. This happens when we first become believers. It's like an evil dictator is overthrown and run out of the country. It's done. Finito. Sin isn't in charge anymore. Jesus is.

But after the regime of sin in our lives has ended, there's still work to be done. As we've seen, the flesh is still active in our lives, and it keeps on fighting. It's as if the deposed dictator still has insurgents in the country who carry out guerrilla warfare in his behalf. So the second stage of cleansing our lives from sin's power involves rooting out the remaining presence and activity of sin in our lives. That's an ongoing process that continues throughout our lives on earth.

Paul helps us see this twofold deliverance in Romans 6.

In verse 2 he wrote that we "died to sin" when we became Christians, and in verse 8 he said, "We have died with Christ." This is something God did for us at the moment of our salvation. Nothing we do after that can add to or subtract from the fact that sin is no longer in charge of our lives. It's a done deal. The dictator is gone.

But then, in verse 12, Paul urged us to "let not sin therefore reign in your mortal body, to make you obey its passions." How can sin possibly reign if we have died to it? Here Paul was referring to the continued presence and ceaseless activity of sin in the flesh — that left-over guerrilla presence that keeps fighting for control.

We experience the struggle between the desires of the flesh and the desires of the Spirit every day of our lives. And putting that stubborn sin to death is the work of a lifetime (see Romans 8:13). Sometimes it feels like we're not making any progress at all. Or sometimes it seems that we've turned a corner, only to find that we've merely gone around the block and are facing the same sin once again. Guerrilla sins can become entrenched and resistant, and sometimes we feel powerless against them.

But we're not.

You may be thinking, *It's fine to be told sin no longer has rule over me, but it sure doesn't feel that way in my daily life. How can I even hope to see progress?*

Paul supplied an answer in Galatians 5:16: "Walk by the Spirit, and you will not gratify the desires of the flesh."

To walk by the Spirit is to live under the controlling influence of the Holy Spirit and in dependence upon Him. This is the only way we can resist the remaining presence and activity of sin in our lives. It's the only answer to our ongoing power struggle with guerrilla sin.

But what does this mean in practical terms? *How* do we go about walking with the Spirit?

Spending time in the Bible helps. The more we expose our minds to Scripture, the better our ability to understand God's laws and "hear" what the Spirit wants from us.

Prayer is essential too. We need to pray continually for the Spirit's direction and the power to do what we need to do. We need to listen as well, taking the time to be quiet, allowing time for the still, small voice of the Spirit to reach our spiritual ears.

And then . . . we do our best. We try to make right decisions and act in obedience to what we have learned, trusting that the Spirit will make all this possible and that when — not if! — we mess up, we will be forgiven and strengthened to keep trying.

There's an important principle of the Christian life involved here. I call it *dependent responsibility.* It means we are responsible before God to obey His Word and to put to death the sins in our lives, both the so-called acceptable sins and the obviously unacceptable ones. We have to make choices — to do something. At the same time, there's no way we can do this by ourselves. We have to rely on the enabling power of the Holy Spirit. So we are both responsible and dependent. Dealing with the guerrilla sin in our lives is both up to us, in the sense that we keep fighting and trying, and not up to us, in the sense that we are never left to do this alone. Over time, if we persist, we will see the Spirit working in us and through us to cleanse us from the remaining power of sin in our lives.

You may notice, by the way, that biblical writers sometimes speak of God the Father or Jesus the Son as doing this work in us. That's not a contradiction. All three members of the divine Trinity are involved in our spiritual transformation, but the Father and the Son work through the Holy Spirit, who dwells in us (see 1 Corinthians 6:19). For example, Paul prayed to the Father that we will be strengthened with power *through His Spirit* in our inner being (see Ephesians 3:16). So when I speak of the power of the Holy Spirit, I am speaking of the power of the Father, Son, and Holy Spirit as it is worked out in us by the Spirit.

How exactly does the Spirit work in our lives? The process can be mysterious. We won't always be able to comprehend or explain it. But if we persist, bathing our minds in Scripture and prayer and doing our best to live obediently, we will begin to see evidence of what He is doing in our lives. Here are just a few of the ways this may happen.

First, the Spirit may convict us of sin. That is, we'll become aware that a particular action or attitude or pattern is sinful and that we need to do something about it. The Spirit does this through Scripture, which He inspired (see 2 Timothy 3:16). He works through our consciences as they are enlightened and sensitized by exposure to His Word. I have even known Him to bring a specific act to my memory and use that to point out a pattern of subtle sin in my life.

But the Spirit doesn't just convict us of sin. He also strengthens us to deal with that sin (see Philippians 4:13). We probably won't feel this power, though, until we actually *do* something. We don't just sit around waiting to feel stronger. Instead, we take a step in obedience and the Spirit moves in to help. (It's that responsible dependence again.)

There are also times when the Holy Spirit works in us without our conscious involvement. Hebrews 13:20-21 speaks of God "working in us that which is pleasing in his sight." I find this especially encouraging. Even in our most dismal days, when sin seems to be winning, we can be sure the Holy Spirit is at work behind the scenes. He might even use our setbacks to humble us and cause us to depend on Him more.

The Holy Spirit definitely works for our transformation by arranging events and experiences to challenge us and help us grow. If you are prone to sinful anger, you can be sure you'll encounter circumstances that make you mad. If you tend to be judgmental, you'll probably have plenty of opportunity to judge others or refrain from it. While God does not tempt us to sin (see James 1:13-14), He does bring or allow circumstances that give us opportunity to put our particular subtle sins to death.

Obviously, none of this would work if God wasn't in complete control. But He is! Many passages of Scripture affirm this, but Lamentations 3:37-38 states it most explicitly: "Who has spoken and it came to pass, unless the Lord has commanded it? Is it not from the mouth of the Most High that good and bad come?" The takeaway from this Scripture is that God is indeed in control of our circumstances and can use every event of our lives—often in some mysterious way—to make us more like Jesus.

Step by step, as we walk with the Spirit, the Spirit will set us free.

# YOUR TURN

"Walk by the Spirit, and you will not gratify the desires of the flesh."
(Galatians 5:16)

## ENGAGE

1. Has there been a time in your life when you felt helpless to fight a
   particular sin? Why do you think that was?

   *Yes. I wasn't walking in the Spirit.*

2. What does the term "dependent responsibility" mean? How does it
   apply to the process of getting sin out of your life?

   *I am responsible before God to put to death any sin in my life.*

   *I will get sin out if I'm serious.*

3. This chapter lists four ways that the Spirit often works in our lives.
   What are they? Have you experienced any of these in your own
   life?
   *1 Strengthens us to deal with sin.*
   *2 Behind the scenes*
   *3 arranging events to help me grow*
   *4 Convicts sin*
   *I've experienced all of them*

## ✳ BRING IT TO GOD

Choose a particular sin in your life that has been resisting your efforts
to put it to death. Write out a prayer for the Holy Spirit's guidance and
power as you fight this sin. Write today's date on the prayer and put it
aside until the end of this study.

# CHAPTER 6

# THE DIRECTIONS

So . . . are you ready to get specific about your sneaky sins? In the next section of this book we'll identify some of the most common of these and look at practical ways to fight them. But before we do that, I'd like to make some suggestions for dealing with all of them—a general strategy for battling all our sins, whether scandalous or subtle.

## ANTI-SIN STRATEGY #1: APPLY THE GOSPEL.

I have covered this truth already in chapter 4, but it needs repeating at this point. As soon as we begin to work on an area of sin in our lives, we tend to forget the gospel. We forget that God has already forgiven our sin because of the death of Christ. As Paul wrote in Colossians 2:13-14, He has "forgiven us all our trespasses, by canceling the record of debt that stood against us with its legal demands. This he set aside, nailing it to the cross."

Not only has God forgiven us our sins, He has also credited to us the perfect righteousness of Christ. In every area of life where we have been disobedient, Jesus was perfectly obedient. Are we prone to be anxious? Jesus always perfectly trusted His heavenly Father. Do we have trouble with selfishness? Jesus was always completely self-giving. Are we guilty of unkind words, gossip, or sarcasm? Jesus spoke only those words that would be appropriate for each occasion.

For some thirty-three years, Jesus lived a life of perfect obedience to God, then He culminated that obedience by dying on the cross for our sins. In both His sinless life and His sin-bearing death, Jesus was perfectly righteous, and it is that righteousness that is credited to all who believe (see Romans 3:21-22; Philippians 3:9).

As we struggle to put our subtle sins to death, we must always keep in mind that (1) our sins are forgiven and (2) we are accepted as righteous by God because of the sinless life and the sin-bearing death of our Lord Jesus Christ. There is no greater motivation for dealing with sin in our lives than the realization of these two glorious truths of the gospel.

## ANTI-SIN STRATEGY #2: DEPEND ON THE HOLY SPIRIT.

Again, we have already addressed this truth in detail in chapter 5, but it too bears repeating because we never get beyond our constant need of the Spirit's enabling power. And we forget that so easily! The default setting for most of us is trying to get by with our own willpower, and we're just not up to the task.

Our spiritual life may be compared to the motor of an electric appliance. The motor does the actual work but is constantly dependent upon the external power source of the electricity for its power. Keeping that analogy in mind can relieve us of a lot of unnecessary guilt and stress. It's not all up to us.

## ANTI-SIN STRATEGY #3: RECOGNIZE YOUR RESPONSIBILITY.

While depending on the Holy Spirit, we still need to diligently pursue all practical steps for dealing with our sins. I know it's tricky to balance both these truths: our dependence and our responsibility. Our tendency is to emphasize one to the neglect of the other. Here the wisdom of some of the older writers can help us: "Work as if it all depends on you, and yet trust as if you did not work at all."

## ANTI-SIN STRATEGY #4: IDENTIFY SPECIFIC RESPECTABLE SINS.

This is one of the purposes of the next part of this book. As you work through each chapter, ask the Holy Spirit to help you see if it applies to you. You'll have to be honest, humble, and brave. As you identify a particular sin, give thought to what situations trigger it. Anticipating the circumstances or events that stimulate the sin can help in putting it to death.

## ANTI-SIN STRATEGY #5: MEMORIZE AND APPLY APPROPRIATE SCRIPTURES.

"I have stored up your word in my heart," wrote the psalmist, "that I might not sin against you" (119:11). To *store up* means to lay aside for future need. Some people, for instance, store up nonperishable food, water, batteries, and other supplies to have on hand in the event of a natural disaster or a political disruption.

But how do we store up God's word? First, by reading Scripture and choosing specific passages, then applying it to our lives, especially to our particular sin patterns. And second, by reflecting on those passages, praying over them, and committing them to memory. Unlike canned goods and water, these "stored" Scriptures can both be used in the present and stored in our hearts for those times when we are tempted to indulge our subtle (or even our not-so-subtle) sins.

Memorizing Scripture is no magic bullet. We have to actually apply it. But if we have memorized and prayed over Scriptures that address our subtle sins, the Holy Spirit will bring them to mind in particular situations to warn us, remind us, and guide us in our response to the temptation. As we work through specific sins in the chapters to come, I will recommend certain Scriptures that might be helpful.

## ANTI-SIN STRATEGY #6: CULTIVATE THE PRACTICE OF PRAYER.

We've already talked about prayer, but I also want to single it out here because it is such an important weapon against our respectable sins. It is through prayer that we continually acknowledge the presence of persistent sin patterns in our lives and our need of the Holy Spirit. In my own life, I find I need both planned, consistent prayers in a daily quiet time and short, spontaneous prayers in the face of temptation.

## ANTI-SIN STRATEGY #7: INVOLVE OTHER BELIEVERS.

Scripture tells us that "two are better than one, because they have a good reward for their toil. For if they fall, one will lift up his fellow. But woe to him who is alone when he falls and has not another to lift him up!" (Ecclesiastes 4:9-10). In other words, we believers need each other—especially if we want to make progress in dealing with our sneaky sin. We need to encourage each other, pray for one another, and urge each other on. So don't try to go it alone. Find someone you can trust—a friend or a couple of friends, even a teacher or family member—to share your efforts.

As you seek to apply these directions, remember that your heart is a battleground between the flesh and the Spirit (see Galatians 5:17). In this guerrilla warfare, the flesh will sometimes get the upper hand. In fact, when you zero in on a particular sin to put it to death, your situation may well get worse before it gets better. But don't worry. The Holy Spirit can use even your times of disobedience and defeat to help you see how deeply rooted your subtle sins are and how totally dependent you are on His power to help you. And it will get better, eventually.

It usually happens gradually. Sometimes you'll feel you're making no progress or have even gone backward. And the task will never be completed in this lifetime. But we have God's promise that the Spirit will not abandon the work He has begun: "He who began a good work in you will bring it to completion at the day of Jesus Christ" (Philippians 1:6).

What does that good work look like? Paul described it beautifully in Galatians 5:22-24: "The fruit of the Spirit is love, joy, peace, patience, kindness, goodness, faithfulness, gentleness, self-control. . . . And those who belong to Christ Jesus have crucified the flesh with its passions and desires."

That's the goal: showing more and more Christlike "fruit" in your life now and putting our sin nature to death in the future. That's where you're going when you walk in the Spirit. You can trust Him to get you there.

The most important thing to remember in all this is that no matter how powerful sin seems in your life, no matter how discouraged you might get in fighting your big and little sin issues, the outcome has already been decided.

Christ has *already* paid the penalty for our sins and won forgiveness for us.

He has *already* banished sin as a ruling power in our lives and sent His Holy Spirit to live within us and deal with those guerrilla stragglers.

The transforming message of the gospel is that both sin's guilt and sin's power have been taken care of in your life.

God wins, remember?

Sin loses.

Everything else is just cleanup, no matter how daunting it may seem. And we never, ever have to fight our sins—even the subtle, sneaky, respectable kind—alone!

## YOUR TURN

"He who began a good work in you will bring it to completion at the day of Jesus Christ." (Philippians 1:6)

### ENGAGE

1. Write out the seven general strategies outlined in this chapter for dealing with sin. Based on the chapters you've already read and your own experience, can you think of any that should be added?

   *Apply the gospel, depend on the Holy Spirit, recognize responsibility, identify sin, memorize + apply, pray, involve others.*

2. How might our lives change if we consistently follow these directions whenever we encounter situations that might trigger sins?

   *We'll be more inclined to consult God.*

3. As we ask God to enable us to deal with our sin, what must we "store up" in our hearts (see Psalm 119:11)?

   *scripture passages*

4. Before moving into the next section of this book, where we'll look in some detail at the more common respectable sins, turn to the chart on pages 52–53. Read down the list of sins and check the columns at the right that seem to apply to you. Don't spend a lot of time on your answers for now; just go with your gut. Later we'll look back at the chart and see if anything has changed.

## BRING IT TO GOD

In this space, write out 1 John 1:9 from your favorite translation of the Bible. Memorize this verse and reflect on its personal promise. Write out a brief prayer thanking God for the promise of 1 John 1:9 and what it means to you personally.

Lord, thank you for being faithful to me. I'm not always to You, but I know I can be with your help and strength. Thank you for your forgivness + grace.

# PART TWO

# SIN BY SIN

# ARE YOU A RESPECTABLE SINNER?

Put a check in the appropriate column to indicate how each subtle, sneaky sin applies to you.

| | Not an issue (as far as I know) | Occasionally a problem | Often a problem | Ouch! That's me! |
|---|---|---|---|---|
| **Ungodliness** (You live or act as if God doesn't exist — ch. 7) | X | | | |
| **Anxiousness / worry** (You're always feeling nervous — ch. 8) | | | X | |
| **Frustration** (You're really bothered by anything that gets in your way or disturbs your plans — ch. 8) | | | | X |
| **Discontentment** (You're just not satisfied with your life or your circumstances — ch. 9) | X | X | | |
| **Unthankfulness** (You neglect to give thanks for God's gifts — ch. 10) | X | | | |
| **Unthankfulness in difficult circumstances** (You don't give thanks because you don't *feel* thankful — ch. 10) | | X | | |
| **Self-righteousness** (You think you're a better person than others — ch. 11) | | | X | |
| **Pride of correct belief** (You think you're right and everyone else is wrong — ch. 11) | | | | |
| **Pride of achievements** (You think you deserve recognition because you did it all on your own — ch. 11) | | | | X |
| **An independent spirit** (No one can tell you anything! — ch. 11) | X | | | |
| **Selfishness about interests** (You mostly talk about what you're into — ch. 12) | X | X | | |
| **Time selfishness** (You guard your own time or thoughtlessly impose on others' time — ch. 12) | X | | | |
| **Financial selfishness** (You forget that your money is a gift from God and keep it mostly for yourself — ch. 12) | X | | | |
| **Thoughtlessness** (You're not considerate of others' needs and feelings — ch. 12) | X | | | |
| **Lack of self-control — eating or drinking** (You tend to give in to your desires for certain consumables — ch. 13) | | X | | |
| **Lack of self-control — temper** (You have a hot temper or a short fuse — ch. 13) | | X | | |
| **Lack of self-control — finances** (You're in debt or spend without thought — ch. 13) | X | | | |
| **Impatience** (You respond strongly and often harshly to others' failures — ch. 14) | | X | | |
| **Irritability** (You're quick to be impatient, and you're impatient a lot — ch.14) | X | | | |

| | Not an issue (as far as I know) | Occasionally a problem | Often a problem | Ouch! That's me! |
|---|---|---|---|---|
| **Anger** (You respond to an offense with strong feelings and perhaps antagonism, though your actual actions may vary — ch. 15) | | | | X |
| **Anger at God** (You feel that the Lord has done you wrong — ch. 15) | | X | | |
| **Weeds of anger** (You hold on to resentment, bitterness, hostility, and grudges — ch. 16) | | | | X |
| **A critical spirit** (You are a harsh and chronic fault finder — ch. 17) | X | | | |
| **Envy** (Someone you identify with enjoys an advantage, and you resent it — ch. 18) | | | | X |
| **Jealousy** (Someone threatens your position, and you resent it — ch. 18) | | | | X |
| **Competitiveness** (You feel driven to be on top — ch. 18) | | | X | X |
| **Control** (You'll do almost anything to get your way — ch. 18) | X | | | |
| **Gossip** (You spread rumors about other people — ch. 19) | X | | | |
| **Slander** (You tell deliberate falsehoods about someone else to gain an advantage — ch. 19) | | | | |
| **Lying** (You avoid the truth with direct falsehoods, exaggerations, partial truths, or little white lies — ch. 19) | | X | | |
| **Using hurtful words** (Your speech tends to be harsh, sarcastic, insulting — ch. 19) | | X | | |
| **Financial worldliness** (You handle money just like everyone in the culture — spending instead of giving — ch. 20) | X | | | |
| **Vicarious immorality** (You aren't directly immoral, but you enjoy those who are and tend to go along with the surrounding culture — ch. 20) | | | X | |
| **Practical idolatry** (You put people, things, and activities ahead of God — ch. 20) | | | | X |

# CHAPTER 7

# UNGODLY

How often do you think about God in the course of your everyday life—when you're not at church or at youth group or having your quiet time and family devotions?

If your answer is "not very often," you're like a lot of Christians I know, including myself at times. You participate in the respectable sin of ungodliness.

*What do you mean, ungodliness? I'm a Christian, not some kind of pagan or atheist. I go to church. I've been saved. And yes, I know I sin, but I'm working on that. I'm not that bad a person.*

My point exactly.

You see, most of us get ungodliness and wickedness mixed up. They're not the same thing at all. A person may be a nice person or a good citizen and still be ungodly.

The apostle Paul wrote in Romans 1:18, "The wrath of God is revealed from heaven against all ungodliness and unrighteousness." Note that he distinguished ungodliness from unrighteousness. Unrighteousness refers to sinful thoughts, words, or deeds, but ungodliness describes an attitude toward God. An atheist or avowed secularist is obviously an ungodly person, but so are a lot of morally decent people, even if they believe in God.

Ungodliness basically means living your everyday life with little or no thought of God. God is essentially irrelevant in an ungodly person's life. He just doesn't come up.

We rub shoulders with ungodly people every day during our

ordinary activities. They may be friendly, courteous, and helpful to other people, but God is not at all in their thoughts. They may even attend church for an hour or so each week but then live the remainder of the week as if God doesn't exist. They are not wicked people, but they are ungodly.

The sad fact is that many of us who are believers live that way too. Survey after survey continues to inform us that there is little difference between the values and behavior patterns of Christians and non-Christians. Surely this reflects the fact that we live much of our ordinary lives with little or no thought of God. It's not that we consciously or deliberately put God out of our minds. We may even read our Bibles and pray for a few minutes at the beginning of each day, but then we go out and basically live as though God doesn't exist. We might go for hours without thinking of Him at all. In that sense, we are hardly different from our nice, decent, but unbelieving neighbors.

Consider these words from James: "Come now, you who say, 'Today or tomorrow we will go into such and such a town and spend a year there and trade and make a profit'—yet you do not know what tomorrow will bring. What is your life? For you are a mist that appears for a little time and then vanishes. Instead you ought to say, 'If the Lord wills, we will live and do this or that'" (4:13-15).

James did not condemn these people for making plans or even planning to set up a business and make a profit. What he condemned was that they didn't acknowledge their dependence on God in their planning. And we do that too. We make our plans without recognizing our utter dependence on God to carry them out. That is one expression of ungodliness.

In the same way, we seldom think of our accountability to God and our responsibility to live according to what He has shown us in Scripture. It's not that we are living obviously sinful lives. It's just that we seldom consider what God wants and, for the most part, are content to avoid obvious sins. Yet Paul wrote to the Colossian believers, "We have not ceased to pray for you, asking that you may be filled with the knowledge of his will in all spiritual wisdom and understanding, so as to walk in a manner worthy of the Lord, fully pleasing to him, bearing fruit in every good work and increasing in the knowledge of God" (1:9-10).

Notice how God-centered that prayer is. Paul wanted his hearers to know how God wants us to live. He desired that their lives would be worthy of God and fully pleasing to Him, and he prayed to that end. In short, he wanted the Colossians to be godly people.

How does Paul's prayer for the Colossians compare with our prayers for ourselves, our families, and our friends? Do our prayers reflect a concern for God's will and God's glory and a desire that our lives will be pleasing to Him? Or are they more like to-do lists we present to God, asking Him to take care of our needs and those of our family and friends?

Now, it is not wrong to bring these daily concerns to God. In fact, that's one way we can acknowledge our daily dependence on Him. But if that's all we pray about, we are merely treating God as a personal assistant or a genie without a lamp. Our prayers are usually human-centered, not God-centered, and in that sense we are ungodly.

For Paul, all of life is to be lived out in the presence of God with an eye to pleasing Him. Consider what he wrote to those messed-up Corinthians: "Whether you eat or drink, or whatever you do, do all to the glory of God" (1 Corinthians 10:31). The *all* of that sentence includes every activity of our days. We are not only to eat to the glory of God, we are to drive to the glory of God . . . and shop to the glory of God . . . and study to the glory of God . . . and text and tweet and hang out to the glory of God. Everything we do is to be done to the glory of God. That is the mark of a godly person.

Doing all to God's glory means that I live every day with a twofold goal.

First, I want God to be pleased with the way I go about the ordinary activities of my day and, obviously, not displeased with anything I think or say or do. So I pray prospectively over the day before me, asking that the Holy Spirit will direct my thoughts, words, and actions to be pleasing to Him.

Second, I desire that all my daily activities will honor God before other people. Jesus said, "Let your light shine before others, so that they may see your good works and give glory to your Father who is in heaven" (Matthew 5:16). By contrast, Paul wrote to the self-righteous Jews in Rome, "You who boast in the law dishonor God by breaking the law. For, as it is written, 'The name of God is blasphemed among the Gentiles because of you'" (Romans 2:23-24).

Think of it this way: If everyone you interact with in the course of an ordinary day knows that you trust in Christ as Savior and Lord and represent Him in the world, would they get a good impression of Him by interacting with you? Or would you perhaps be like the father whose child said, "If God is like my father, I want nothing to do with God"?

Hopefully not many of us would be like that father. But how far do we go in a positive direction to improve His reputation? Do we consciously and prayerfully seek His glory in all we say and do in our most ordinary activities of the day? Or do we actually go about those activities with little or no thought of God?

An even more telling indicator of our tendency toward ungodliness is our meager desire to develop an intimate relationship with God. Biblical writers clearly yearned for such a relationship:

*As a deer pants for flowing streams,*
*    so pants my soul for you, O God.*
*My soul thirsts for God,*
*    for the living God.*
*When shall I come and appear before God? (Psalm 42:1-2)*

*One thing have I asked of the LORD . . .*
*that I may dwell in the house of the LORD*
*    all the days of my life,*
*to gaze upon the beauty of the LORD. (Psalm 27:4)*

Yet how many of us claim those desires? A person may be moral and upright, or even busy in Christian service, yet have little or no desire to draw close to God. This is a mark of ungodliness.

If you have followed me this far, you can see that there is still some degree of ungodliness in all of us. The question is: *How much? How much of my life do I live without any regard for God? What percentage of my daily activities have no reference to Him?*

Total godliness and utter ungodliness are the opposite ends of a continuum. All of us are somewhere between those two extremes. The only person who ever lived a totally godly life was Jesus, and probably no true believer lives a totally ungodly life. But where are you on the spectrum? As you consider this, remember that we are not talking about righteous versus wicked behavior. We are talking about living as if God is relevant or irrelevant.

Many people believe that the sin of pride underlies most other sins. But I have decided that ungodliness is even more basic than pride. In fact, I believe that all our other acceptable sins can ultimately be traced to this root sin of ungodliness. If we change our ungodly patterns of living, then, it can have a positive effect on our other sins.

Think how it would curb our pride, for example, if we consciously lived every day in the awareness that all we are, all we have, and all we accomplish is by the grace of God. How could we possibly look down on others? Or think of how much more careful our speech would be if we spoke in awareness that God hears every word. Talking sins such as gossip or lying simply could not thrive.

So how do we deal with our sin of ungodliness and become more godly in our daily lives? Paul suggested an answer in his words to Timothy: "Train yourself for godliness" (1 Timothy 4:7). The athletic metaphor implies commitment, consistency, discipline, and focus. Paul wanted Timothy and all believers of every age to be just as committed to growth in godliness and just as intentional in pursuing it as an athlete training for a championship. But how many of us actually think that way?

I can't help but contrast our anemic desire for godliness with the attitude of young men in our city who recently camped out all night in snow and cold at an electronics store to buy one of a limited supply of the newest gaming system. Some arrived at 9:30 on a Saturday morning to wait for the doors to open at 8 a.m. Sunday. What would our lives be like if we had that kind of zeal for godliness?

Our goal in the pursuit of godliness should be to grow in our conscious awareness that every moment of our lives is lived in the presence of God, that we are responsible to Him and dependent on Him. This goal would include a growing desire to please Him and glorify Him in the most ordinary activities of life.

Because ungodliness is so all-encompassing, it might be helpful to identify specific areas of life where you tend to live without regard to God. These might include school, computer time, hanging out with your friends, playing or watching sports, even your driving. Scripture texts that might be helpful to memorize, ponder, and pray over include 1 Timothy 4:7-8; 1 Corinthians 10:31; Colossians 1:9-10; 3:23; Psalm 42:1-2; 63:1; 27:4.

Above all, pray that God will help you remember that you live every moment of every day under His all-seeing eye. This is a good word for all of us. For while He might not be on our minds, we are certainly on His. He sees every deed we do, hears every word we say, and knows every thought we think (see Psalm 139:1-4). He even searches out our motives.

Let us then seek to be as mindful of Him as He is of us.

# YOUR TURN

"The grace of God has appeared, bringing salvation for all people, training us to renounce ungodliness." (Titus 2:11-12)

## ENGAGE

1. How is the definition of ungodliness at the beginning of this chapter different from what you thought ungodliness meant? What does Romans 1:18 reveal about this common sneaky sin?

   *Ungodliness is not letting God be a part of your life – I always thought it was being pagan + saying there is not God.*
   *– God's wrath will come upon you.*

2. Reread 1 Corinthians 10:31 and Matthew 5:16. To what extent are you mindful of doing "all" to the glory of God? How has ungodliness crept (or marched) into your social relationships . . . ordinary activities . . . prayers . . . daily planning?

   *God isn't in them.*

3. What practical things can we do each day to "train" ourselves "for godliness" (1 Timothy 4:7) so that we please and glorify God during even ordinary activities? *Commit scripture to memory. Be in His word more + learn about ungodliness.*
   *For me, I didn't realize ungodliness was as big an issue as it is.*

## BRING IT TO GOD

Ask God to kindle within you an even stronger desire to live a lifestyle of godliness and thankfulness.

# CHAPTER 8

# ANXIOUS AND FRUSTRATED

Some years ago, I went through the entire New Testament looking for teaching on and examples of various character traits. I found twenty-seven.

It may not surprise you that *love* was the big winner. It came up at least fifty times.

*Humility* was a close second, with forty instances.

But what really surprised me is what came third: *trust in God*. It's stressed at least thirteen times in the New Testament. To me that means (1) trust is a big issue for a lot of people and (2) God really wants us to learn to trust Him.

The opposite of trust in God is anxiety, and Jesus had a lot to say about that. In Matthew 6:25-34, for instance, He used the word *anxious* or *worry* six times. We're not to be anxious about having something to eat, drink, or wear, and we're not supposed to worry about what's going to happen in the future. Jesus also told us repeatedly to "fear not" (see, for example, Matthew 10:31; Luke 12:7). Paul picked up the same theme in Philippians 4:6: "Do not be anxious about anything." And Peter urged, "[Cast] all your anxieties on him, because he cares for you" (1 Peter 5:7).

When you or I say to someone, "Don't be anxious" or "Don't be afraid," we are usually just trying to encourage that person. But when Jesus says it (or Paul or Peter, by divine inspiration), it's a command.

In other words, *anxiety is sin.*

Does that surprise you? It surprises a lot of people because anxiety seems so . . . normal. It's often dismissed as a matter of temperament (as in "anxious personality") or an inevitable response to difficult events in a fallen world. It's true that there's a lot of anxiety going around, but that doesn't mean it's normal or inevitable. It certainly doesn't mean anxiety isn't a sin. Can you picture Jesus ever being anxious or frustrated? And aren't we supposed to model our lives on Him?

Anxiety is sinful because it's basically distrusting God. I get anxious because, at some level, I just don't believe God will take care of me. Suppose someone you love were to tell you, "I don't trust you. I don't believe you love me and will care for me." You'd be insulted, right? Yet that is what we are saying to God by our anxiety.

Anxiety also reveals disbelief in or resistance to God's providence. Providence simply means that God's in charge of everything that happens. He has a plan. He orchestrates everything in His universe for His glory and the good of His people. Some believers have difficulty believing that, and those who do believe often lose sight of it or resist it. We tend to focus on the immediate causes of our anxiety rather than remembering that it's all under God's control.

This is a persistent struggle for me when it comes to air travel. I fly often for speaking engagements, and my travel usually involves a connecting flight from the city where I live to one of the airline's hub cities. If that first flight is late, I may miss the next flight to my destination. Then I am tempted to become anxious about making that connection, because usually I am scheduled to speak within a few hours after my scheduled arrival, and it's important to me that I make that flight so I can get comfortably settled before it's time to speak.

But what if God's agenda is different from mine? What if He has a reason for me to be late for that meeting or miss it altogether? Will I fret and fume, or will I believe that God is in control of my travel and accept *His* agenda, whatever that may be?

I tend to think, *Lord, it's important that I arrive in time to speak at that meeting. The people in charge are counting on me. What will they do if I don't arrive in time?* But I am learning to add, *God, it's Your meeting. If You don't want me there, that's Your business. And what the people who are counting on me to be there will do is also Your business. God, I accept Your agenda for this situation, whatever that may be.*

Accepting that God's in control does not mean we shouldn't pray about our concerns. Paul's command to not be anxious is accompanied by the instruction to pray about whatever situation is bothering us (see Philippians 4:6). And even Jesus, anticipating His suffering on the cross, prayed, "If it be possible, let this cup pass from me; nevertheless, not as I will, but as you will" (Matthew 26:39). So it is appropriate to pray for relief and for deliverance from whatever triggers our anxiety. But we should always do so with an attitude of accepting whatever God may have in mind and a confidence that, whatever the outcome, God's plan is better than ours.[1]

Do you, like me, tend to get anxious in certain circumstances? Do you tend to chafe under God's agenda when it is different from your own? If so, I encourage you to memorize and pray over some of the Scriptures mentioned above. They really help.

Above all, ask God to help you believe that He really does know better than you do. His will for you in any circumstance comes from His infinite wisdom and goodness and is intended for your good. Ask Him to give you a heart that is submissive to Him even when His plans conflict with yours.

## WORRY

Worry is a synonym for anxiety in the Bible. In popular usage, however, we tend to associate worry with more long-term difficult or painful circumstances for which there appears to be no resolution. These are the kinds of circumstances that tend to keep us up stewing over what might happen and trying to figure out what to do.

I have several friends who have mentally or physically dependent adult children. The parents are getting older. And they can easily lie awake at night wondering, *Who will care for my child after I die?* If I were them, I'd be tempted to worry too. And yet the Bible tells us, "Do not worry about tomorrow" (Matthew 6:34, NIV).

We do have the promises of God and the ministry of the Holy Spirit to help us in these difficult times. Recently, a friend who is actually experiencing one of these long-term situations called my attention to the J. B. Phillips translation of 1 Peter 5:7: "You can throw the whole weight of your anxieties upon him, for you are his personal concern." Jesus said that God does not forget a single sparrow (see Luke 12:6). It's not a stretch to say that you, His child, are indeed His personal concern.

Granted, that's not always easy to remember, though. Sometimes a situation we're facing looms larger in our minds than the promises of God. Trust in God's care and belief in His providence can be a struggle. At such times I find it helpful to think of the distressed father in the Bible whose son was possessed by demons. "I believe," he cried out to Jesus, "help my unbelief!" (Mark 9:24).

There is a vast difference between stubborn unbelief such as was demonstrated by the people of Jesus' hometown (see Mark 6:5-6) and the struggling faith of the son's father. God honors our struggles, and the Holy Spirit will help us. The important issue is that we seek to honor God through whatever faith we have and lean on Him to help us.

## FRUSTRATION

Closely akin to anxiety or worry is the sin of frustration. Whereas anxiety involves fear, frustration usually involves being upset or even angry at whatever or whoever is blocking our plans. For instance, I might have an important document to print from my computer, but the printer will only produce gobbledygook. My blood pressure begins to rise. I get frustrated.

Actually, this type of reaction has its roots in ungodliness, the tendency to live as if God were not involved in my life or my circumstances. I fail to recognize the invisible hand of God behind whatever is triggering my frustration. In the heat of the moment, I tend not to think about God at all. Instead, I focus entirely on the immediate cause of my frustration—my printer.

The passage of Scripture that has greatly helped me deal with frustration is Psalm 139:16, which says, "All the days ordained for me were written in your book before one of them came to be" (NIV). "Days ordained for me" refers not only to the length of my life, but to all my daily events and circumstances. God is in charge of each one of them. I can trust Him to work things out for His glory and my good.

I find this is a tremendously encouraging and comforting thought. When something happens that threatens to frustrate me, I actually quote Psalm 139:16 to myself and then say to God, "This circumstance is part of Your plan for my life today. Help me to respond to it in faith and in a God-honoring way. And please give me wisdom to know what to do."

Note what resources I have brought to bear on the circumstance that tempted me to frustration. First, I've applied a specific Scripture to the circumstance. Second, I've asked for the Spirit's help in responding in a godly manner—that is, without the sin of frustration. Finally, I've asked for practical wisdom. After all, my document does need to be printed!

I have also found it beneficial to ask God if there is something I need to learn or pay attention to. Sometimes God uses events that tempt us toward frustration to get our attention or even to give us a nudge in an area we need to grow in.

In any case, there are no events in our lives that do not ultimately come to us from the invisible hand of God, nothing that is beyond His loving care.

We really can trust Him. Why worry?

## YOUR TURN

"Humble yourselves, therefore, under the mighty hand of God . . . casting all your anxieties on him, because he cares for you." (1 Peter 5:6-7)

## ENGAGE

1. Read Matthew 6:25-34 and make a list of the things Jesus said we shouldn't be anxious about. What did He say about how we should respond to anxiety (worry)? *He says God already knows about this worry + to seek 1st the kingdom of God + His righteousness, and all things will be added*

2. Why does anxiety seem so normal in our culture—in our daily *2you.* activities, in advertising, in news reports? How does the Bible's teaching about anxiety contradict what modern culture assumes about it? *Our culture is always looking to be safe + healthy + rich ~ when we look to worry + ourselves, the focus is turned from God. - Anxiety is a*

3. Do you believe that some people are naturally more prone to *disease* anxiety or frustration than others? Can a natural reaction still be a sin? *Yes. It depends on the reaction, but yes, it can still be a sin.*

4. What circumstances tend to make you anxious? Worried? Frustrated? How have you typically reacted? How does your typical reaction compare to what this chapter recommends?

*The future; I normally try to handle it on my own, but now more + more I bring it to God. →Definite failure←*

## BRING IT TO GOD

Choose one circumstance that concerns you right now and tempts you to anxiety, worry, or frustration. Picture yourself laying that circumstance at God's feet and leaving it there for Him to handle. Then thank God that you can always trust Him to care for you.

1. your life — eat, drink, wear
2. Clothing
3. Tomorrow (the future)

# CHAPTER 9

# DISCONTENT

Anxiety is a fearful uncertainty over the future—what might happen. Frustration is usually the result of some immediate event that has blocked my plans or desires. Discontentment, the subject of this chapter, most often arises from ongoing and unchanging circumstances we can do little or nothing about.

Have you ever heard anyone say, "I hate my life"? That's usually an exaggeration, but it's also the essence of sinful discontentment. Discontented people tend to be disgruntled, dissatisfied, and generally unhappy.

Not all discontentment is sinful, of course. All of us should, to some degree, be discontent with our spiritual growth. If we are not, we will stop growing. There is also what we might call a prophetic discontentment with injustice and other evils in society that is coupled with a desire to see positive change. Even discontentment over personal circumstances can be a gift from God that motivates us to change those circumstances. But when chronic unhappiness about our circumstances poisons our relationship with God, it definitely becomes a sin.

Actually, the most frequent warnings in Scripture against discontentment concern money and possessions—being discontent with what we have. But more common among committed Christians, I believe, is discontentment triggered by personal circumstances:

- A physical deformity or disability
- Living with divorced or alcoholic parents

- A learning disability
- Unemployment or an unfulfilling job
- Singleness (when you want to be married)

Such situations are extremely painful, but discontentment can also involve trivial circumstances. For instance, I'm not good at administrative details, so having to constantly deal with them tempts me to be discontent. I am personally acquainted with some of those more difficult areas too. All my life I have had both a visual and a hearing disability, neither of which is treatable. I can remember the feeling of rejection as I was growing up when, because of my visual disability, I could not play baseball like the other boys. Still today, even as an older adult, I find those lifetime disabilities often make life inconvenient, if not difficult.

And yes, I know these problems of mine are minor indeed compared to what many believers experience. I just want you to know that if you struggle with discontentment, I'm right there with you. At any rate, it is our response to our circumstances rather than how difficult they are that determines whether or not we are discontented.

Whatever situation tempts us to be discontented, we need to recognize that discontentment, like anxiety or frustration, is sin. We are so used to responding to difficult circumstances with anxiety, frustration, or discontentment that we consider them normal reactions. But that's part of the problem with sneaky sins: We don't recognize them. Our response to them, in fact, may be no different than that of unbelievers who never factor God into their situations. So we are back to our ungodliness as the root cause of our sins.

In the previous chapter I mentioned that Psalm 139:16 helps me a lot with frustration. It helps me with discontentment as well. Whatever our circumstances, and however difficult they may be, the truth is that they are ordained by God as part of His overall plan for our lives. God does nothing and allows nothing without a purpose. And His purposes, however mysterious they may be to us, are always for His glory and our ultimate good.

And for those of us who face physical disabilities or even physical-appearance issues, Psalm 139:13 can be helpful as well: "You formed my inward parts; you knitted me together in my mother's womb." God so directed our DNA and other biological factors that determine our physical makeup that the psalmist could say, "God formed me in my mother's womb."

That is an incredible thought! You and I are who we are physically because that is the way God made us. And He made us the way we are because that is how we can best fulfill His plan for our lives. For those with severe disabilities, that truth may be hard to take. But if we believe that we are who we are and what we are because that is the way God made us, then we have to believe He can use those disabilities to glorify Himself.

Obviously, many areas of life are not addressed by Psalm 139:13. But you can be sure you will be able to find specific Scriptures or principles that will address your particular circumstances.

Years ago a friend gave me a long poem by Amy Carmichael called "In Acceptance Lieth Peace." There's a lot of wisdom in it for those of us who struggle with sinful discontentment. The poem basically describes different ways a man attempts to deal with his pain. First he tries putting behind him all the bad things that have happened. Then he tries to distract himself by staying busy. He attempts to withdraw from other people and simply give up. Nothing helps. Finally the man just chooses to accept his pain and finds the peace and contentment he is looking for.

Acceptance basically means adopting a position of honest trust regarding our difficulties. We don't pretend they're not real or painful. We don't try to forget them or run from them. We simply give over to God our ideas of what should happen, trusting that He knows what is best for us and purposes only that.

To me, this posture of acceptance is summed up by an anonymous verse a friend sent me after my first wife died. Both in those days of grief and in the years since then, this little verse has helped me handle my sins of discontentment:

*Lord, I am willing to:*
*Receive what You give,*
*Lack what You withhold,*
*Relinquish what You take.*

You will recognize that there is a recurring theme running through this chapter as well as the previous one: the supreme power (often called sovereignty), wisdom, and goodness of God in all the circumstances of our lives.[1] Whether those circumstances are short-term or long-term, our ability to respond to them in a God-honoring manner depends on our ability and willingness to trust God in the midst of them. And we must do this by faith, believing that the Bible's teaching really is true and that God has brought or allowed these difficult circumstances in our lives for His glory and our ultimate good.

You may ask, "But shouldn't I pray for physical healing or for relief from any other painful circumstance?" Yes, we are invited to pray about these circumstances and also to do what we can reasonably do to change them. But we should do these things in confidence that our infinitely wise and loving heavenly Father knows what is best for us. And if God answers our prayers with a no, we must be willing to accept that.

Finally, I realize that in dealing with discontentment, I probably have touched some raw nerves. You may be thinking, *If he knew what I'm going through, he wouldn't be so glib and preachy.* It's true that I don't know your situation, but I assure you I'm not being glib. I do write as one who has struggled with discontentment and sought to overcome it with the truths I've set forth in this chapter. They have helped me, and I pray they will help you.

May all of us, with the help of the Holy Spirit, move from any negative attitudes of discontentment to a positive attitude of being stewards of the difficult and disappointing circumstances God has given us so that we may somehow glorify Him in all of life.

## YOUR TURN

"All the days ordained for me were written in your book before one of them came to be." (Psalm 139:16, NIV)

**ENGAGE**

*my relationship w/ God*

*→ Chronic unhappiness that poisons*

1. What is discontentment? When does it spur us to positive action, and when is it sinful? *ongoing circumstances I can do nothing about. when God sets it there to show us to change; when we are concerned for money or possessions or disabilities that hinder spiritual growth*

2. The author writes, "It is our response to our circumstances rather than how difficult they are that determines whether or not we are discontented." Do you agree or disagree? Why?

   *yes I agree – everyone has a choice to make.*

3. Do you think God sometimes allows us to face difficult, unchanging circumstances for reasons we may never know? Feel free to share a personal example if you know one. *yes. Robert*

4. Throughout this book, the author encourages us to remember God's attributes. If we believe and remember that God is infinitely wise, loving, and knows what is best for us, then how will we respond to circumstances that tempt us to be discontented? On the other hand, if we think God is simply toying with us and wanting us to suffer, how will we respond to trials?

   *we will be content and happy. Ultimately, we'll grow spiritually + mentally → we'll digress..*

## BRING IT TO GOD

Pray for yourself the prayer of relinquishment mentioned in this chapter:

> *Lord, I am willing to:*
> *Receive what You give,*
> *Lack what You withhold,*
> *Relinquish what You take.*

# CHAPTER 10

# UNTHANKFUL

In Jesus' day, leprosy was a terrible disease to have. Its victims not only became disfigured, they were also outcasts. No one would come near them. In fact, Moses' law required that people with leprosy had to cry out, "Unclean, unclean," wherever they went so people would know to stay away (see Leviticus 13:45). It was a sad, lonely existence.

One day while Jesus was walking along the road toward Jerusalem, He encountered a group of these sick, lonely men—ten of them. They stood at a distance, as they were supposed to, and begged Him to help them. And He did. He told them to go and show themselves to the priests, who were the ones who could officially pronounce lepers cleansed. And as the sick men went to do this, they realized they were completely healed.

Can you imagine how thrilled those men were? They must have been jumping up and down with glee. But only one of them—one man out of ten—bothered to go back to tell Jesus thank you (see Luke 17:11-19).

*That's pretty bad*, we think. *How could those nine men be so ungrateful? Jesus healed them from a horrible disease that was ruining their lives. They could at least have said thank you!*

And yet far too many of us are guilty of the same sin of unthankfulness.

Spiritually speaking, our condition was once far worse than the physical disease of leprosy. We were not diseased, but spiritually dead. We were slaves to the world, to Satan, and to the passions of our own sinful nature. But God, in His great mercy and love, reached out to us and gave us spiritual life (see Ephesians 2:1-5).

That's a far greater miracle, with infinitely greater benefits, than healing from leprosy. Yet how often do we give thanks for our salvation? Have you stopped today to express heartfelt gratitude to God for delivering you from the domain of darkness and transferring you to the kingdom of His Son?

The truth is, we owe God thanks for our very lives. Paul said that God Himself "gives to all mankind life and breath and everything" (Acts 17:25). That means that every breath we draw is a gift from God. Everything we are and everything we have is a gift from Him. And you know that, of course, but how often do you stop to give Him thanks?

At the end of a day at school, do you ever take time to say, "Thank you, heavenly Father, for giving me the ability and opportunity to prepare for my future life?"

Do you sit in your room and look around and say to God, "Everything here is a gift from You. Thank You!"?

When you play tennis or sing in the praise band or mix paint, do you ever stop to thank God for the talents you were born with and the skills you've been able to acquire?

Do you ever ride your bike or skateboard through the park and shout thanks into the wind for the trees and the sky and the ability to move?

And when you give thanks at mealtime, is it routine and perfunctory, or is it a heartfelt expression of your gratitude to God that He provides for all your physical needs?

Taking for granted all the blessings that God has so richly bestowed on us and failing to continually give Him thanks is one of our "acceptable" sins. In fact, far too many Christians wouldn't think of it as sin. Yet Paul, in his description of a Spirit-filled person, said we are to "[give] thanks always and for everything to God the Father in the name of our Lord Jesus Christ" (Ephesians 5:20).

Note the words *always* and *everything*. That means our whole lives should be ones of continually giving thanks.

Giving thanks to God for both His temporal and spiritual blessings in our lives is not just a nice thing to do. It is something we are commanded to do. As God warned the Israelites, "Beware lest you say in your heart, 'My power and the might of my hand have gotten me this wealth.' You shall remember the LORD your God, for it is he who gives you power to get wealth, that he may confirm his covenant that he swore to your fathers, as it is this day" (Deuteronomy 8:17-18).

Failure to "remember" the Lord and give Him the thanks due Him is sin, an affront and an insult to the One who created us and sustains us every second of our lives. And if, as Jesus so clearly stated, loving God with all our heart, soul, and mind is the great and first commandment, then failure to give thanks to God as a habit of life is a violation of the greatest commandment.

In Romans 1:18-32, Paul described the downward moral spiral he observed in pagan society of that day—everything from gossip to perverted sex and murder. How did it all begin? Paul told us in verse 21: "Although they knew God, they did not honor him as God *or give thanks to him*, but they became futile in their thinking, and their foolish hearts were darkened" (verse 21, italics mine). These people's ever-increasing wickedness actually began with their ungodliness (failure to honor God as God) and their unthankfulness to Him. Their moral degradation was a result of God's judgment on them as He progressively gave them over to the inclinations of their hearts.

And here's the scary thing: Paul's description of the Romans' moral depravity could be applied to our society with hardly a change of words. I can't help but wonder if we're also suffering God's judgment for our failure to honor Him and give Him thanks. And we Christians contribute to this situation, along with society at large, as we fail to give God the thanks we owe. In fact, we may be more guilty because we should know better. That's still another reason for us to practice giving thanks to God always and for everything.

We should especially give thanks when we have experienced an unusual provision from God or deliverance from some difficult circumstance. While working on this chapter, for instance, I flew to São Paulo, Brazil, for a ministry opportunity. After clearing customs, I went to the baggage claim area along with more than 150 other passengers from my flight. Now I should tell you that I'm usually tempted with anxiety at this point because I've had so many delayed-bag incidents. And sure enough, my bag didn't appear. The pressure began to build as bag after bag went by on the conveyor belt, and mine was not among them. I did not want to have to deal with a lost bag in a foreign country.

Finally, after about two-thirds of the passengers had retrieved their luggage, my bag appeared. As I pulled my bag off the conveyor belt, I lifted a heartfelt prayer of thanksgiving to God. I did it again as I unpacked in my hotel room.

Now a delayed-bag incident may seem trivial to you, and in the course of a lifetime it is. But when you have to wear the same clothes for two or three days and replace toiletry articles in a foreign drugstore with unfamiliar currency and a language you don't know, it doesn't seem trivial at all. I was *very* grateful to have my bag that day.

Life is full of events that delay us, inconvenience us, or obstruct or block some plan of ours. In the midst of these events, as I have explained, we should fight against anxiety and frustration. But when God does bring relief or when we see Him deliver us from the possibility of such an event, we should make it a special point to give Him thanks.

## IN ALL CIRCUMSTANCES?

Let's pursue the baggage-claim scenario a bit further. Suppose my bag did not arrive with me on the flight or it never arrived. Should I *still* have given thanks?

Before we look at the answer to that question, mentally insert into this story some predicament of your own, either an actual event or some imaginary one you hope never happens. This will help keep the following answer to the question from being theoretical.

So the question is *Are we to give God thanks when the events do not turn out as we had hoped?* The answer is yes. Paul told us in 1 Thessalonians 5:18, "Give thanks in all circumstances; for this is the will of God in Christ Jesus for you."

But note that this command is different from the one in Ephesians 5:20 that tells us to give thanks to God for *everything*. I believe, considering the context, that in Ephesians, Paul was exhorting us to develop a habit of continual thanksgiving for all the blessings God so graciously pours out on us. He was describing one characteristic of a Spirit-filled life: a thankful heart.

In the Thessalonians passage, however, Paul instructed us to give thanks *in* all circumstances, presumably even those we don't *feel* thankful about. Was Paul asking us to give thanks by sheer willpower when in our heart of hearts we are truly disappointed? The answer to the question lies in the promises of God found in Romans 8:28-29: "We know that for those who love God all things work together for good, for those who are called according to his purpose. For those whom he foreknew he also predestined to be conformed to the image of his Son."

Note that first line: "For those who love God all things work together for good." The meaning is that *God causes* all things to work together for good. "Things"—that is, circumstances—don't work together for good themselves; rather, God directs the outcome of those circumstances for our good.

And what is the "good" anyway? It's defined a little further down: being conformed to the image of God's Son. God intends to use all our circumstances, good and bad (but in the context Paul had in mind, especially the bad ones), to make us more and more like Jesus.

So in situations that do not turn out the way we hoped, we are to intentionally give God thanks that He will use the situation in some way to develop our Christian character. We don't know exactly *how* He might use it, for God's ways are often mysterious and beyond our understanding. So we do it by faith. Trusting in the promise of

God as explained in Romans 8:28-29, we obey the command of 1 Thessalonians 5:18 to give thanks in the circumstances.

Further, as we are in the midst of a difficult circumstance, we have the promise of Romans 8:38-39: "For I am sure that neither death nor life, nor angels nor rulers, nor things present nor things to come, nor powers, nor height nor depth, nor anything else in all creation, will be able to separate us from the love of God in Christ Jesus our Lord."

Again, we must cling to this promise by faith. But if we can do that, we have a dual assurance that enables us to give thanks in this particular difficulty. First, by faith we believe God is using or will use it to make us more like Jesus. Second, we believe that even in the midst of it all, we are enveloped in God's love.

So the giving of thanks in a disappointing or difficult situation is not a matter of gritted teeth and sheer willpower. It is always to be done by faith in the promises of God. If we do that, we are giving thanks with our lips *and* with our hearts.

As we cling to the promises of God, we can say, "Father, the circumstance I am in now is difficult and painful. I would not have chosen it, but You in Your love and wisdom chose it for me. You intend it for my good, and so by faith I thank You for the good You are going to do in my life through it. Help me to genuinely believe this and be able to thank You from my heart."

## YOUR TURN

"Be filled with the Spirit . . . giving thanks always and for everything to God the Father in the name of our Lord Jesus Christ."
(Ephesians 5:18,20)

### ENGAGE

1. Make a list of at least five blessings God has given you. Why is it
   important for us to thank Him for these blessings and make such
   thankfulness a natural part of our lives?

   *family, friends,*
   *School, talent, home*
   → *because we are commanded to*
   *give thanks in everything.*

2. Where does the faith come from to believe and thank God even
   in the midst of difficult circumstances, when you don't *feel*
   thankful?

   *From God's love in Christ Jesus*

3. Describe a challenging time when you were—or were not—able
   to give thanks. What did God teach you through that experience?

   *I wasn't able to give thanks when*
   *I moved. In life, things are*
   *going to change + He is sovereign.*

4. What are some practical ways you can be sure to take time each
   day to thank God for His daily provision and spiritual blessings?

   → *Every breath I take is a*
   *remembrance.*
   → *Constant talk with God*

### BRING IT TO GOD

Raise your own prayer of thanksgiving to God, thanking Him for the
gift of your life and specifically for the five (or more) items on your list.

# CHAPTER 11

# PROUD

He's one of the bad guys of the Bible, the kind people love to hate because he's just so obnoxious. You'll find him in Luke 18: a self-righteous Pharisee who stands in the middle of a public place and prays, "God, I thank you that I am not like other men, extortioners, unjust, adulterers, or even"—he points!—"like this tax collector" (verse 11).

What a jerk! That Pharisee's sin, obviously, was pride, and pride is a major sin in the Bible. It's so important that both James and Peter warned us, "God opposes the proud" (James 4:6; 1 Peter 5:5).

In this chapter, we are going to look at several expressions of pride that are special temptations to believers and most likely to be tolerated sins. But here's something to keep in mind: Whenever we start talking about people like that self-righteous Pharisee, we can easily fall into the same self-righteous attitude that annoys us so much. One of the biggest problems with pride, actually, is that we can see it in others but not in ourselves. So please join me in asking God to reveal to each of us the pride that *He* sees in our lives.

## "I'M BETTER THAN YOU."

The pride of the Pharisee in Jesus' parable was what we can call moral self-righteousness. It expresses itself in assuming that we are better people, morally superior to those around us. This type of pride is not limited to believers. You can find it in any circle of society, around any issue from gun rights to environmental policy. Sadly, it is especially common among conservative, evangelical believers. Why? Because there's so much obvious bad stuff out there—sexual immorality, lying and cheating, drunkenness, drug abuse, abortion, greed, and much more. Because we evangelicals don't (usually) commit those particular sins, we find it easy to look down on those who do.

I'm not saying those sins I've mentioned aren't serious! They are big problems for our society, and I respect those who raise a prophetic voice against them. But if we adopt an attitude of moral self-righteousness in the process, we're falling into sin! In fact, Jesus told the parable about the Pharisee to make that point "to some who trusted in themselves that they were righteous, and treated others with contempt" (Luke 18:9).

I venture that of all the subtle sins we will address in this book, the pride of moral self-righteousness may be the most common, second only to the sin of ungodliness. That may be why it's so difficult to recognize—because we all practice it to some degree. Some people I know seem to get a perverse enjoyment out of discussing how awful society is becoming. They are guilty of the pride of moral superiority. But so are those who roll their eyes over Christians who complain about how awful society is becoming!

Can you see how sneaky this kind of sin really is? It's just so tempting!

So how can we guard against the sin of self-righteousness? First, by reminding ourselves that we're sinners too—that in God's eyes our "respectable" sins are just as bad as those blatant sins we see others doing.

Second, we can adopt the humble attitude of "there but for the grace of God go I." No one is naturally good. We all have to say with David, "Surely I was sinful at birth, sinful from the time my mother conceived me" (Psalm 51:5, NIV). So rather than feeling morally superior to those who practice the sins we condemn, we should feel grateful that God by His grace has kept us from—or perhaps rescued us from—such a lifestyle.

Another way to guard against self-righteous pride can be found in the Old Testament story of Ezra. Ezra was a godly man, a scribe. Yet when he became aware of some deep sin among his people, he chose to identify himself with the people's sin. "My God," he prayed, "I am ashamed and blush to lift my face to you . . . for *our* iniquities have risen higher than *our* heads, and *our* guilt has mounted up to the heavens" (Ezra 9:6, italics mine). Note how Ezra included himself in his confession of guilt: "*our* iniquities" and "*our* guilt." Adopting such an attitude—a sense of "we" instead of "they"—will help protect us from self-righteous pride.

## "I'M RIGHT AND YOU'RE WRONG."

Closely akin to moral pride is pride of correct belief. You could also call this "pride of doctrine." It's basically the attitude that "I'm right and you're wrong."

Don't get tripped up with that word *doctrine*. It simply means "teaching," and it usually refers to a set of teachings that make up a belief system such as Christianity. The trouble is, not all Christians agree on doctrine. Some factions and denominations disagree passionately. And that's when pride of correct belief comes into play. It's not just disagreement. It's an attitude of disdain toward those who disagree with us, a certainty that we're right and they're not only wrong, but also spiritually inferior or even stupid.

This kind of pride can take several forms when it comes to religious belief. Christians may look down on Buddhists or Jews. Baptists may scorn Catholics or Pentecostals. Those who take one side of a theological debate may roll their eyes at the other side. Those who don't care much about doctrine at all may show contempt toward those who do, and vice versa. No one group has a monopoly on this kind of pride.

Paul pinpointed this form of sin when it arose in Corinth over the issue of eating food that had been offered to idols. Some Corinthian Christians were really bothered by this practice, but others insisted that it wasn't a problem. They argued that because they didn't worship the idols, they were free to eat the food. And Paul didn't disagree with them, but he did object to their attitude.

"Now concerning food offered to idols," he wrote, "we know that 'all of us possess knowledge.' This 'knowledge' puffs up, but love builds up" (1 Corinthians 8:1). Paul didn't question their "knowledge"—their conviction that eating food offered to idols was not a problem. But he called them on their pride of correct belief and urged them to adopt an attitude of love instead.

Am I suggesting that correct belief doesn't matter or that we shouldn't defend our strong convictions? No. I believe we should all seek to understand Scripture and know what we believe in. But we should hold our convictions with humility and respect, realizing that many thoughtful and godly people believe differently.

We're all human and humans make mistakes, so there's always the possibility we could be wrong. But even if we're right, being "puffed up" with pride makes us wrong . . . and sinful.

## "LOOK AT ME!"

The Scriptures teach that there is generally a cause-and-effect relationship between hard work and success in any endeavor, whether in academics, athletics, business, or profession. For example, Proverbs 13:4 says, "The soul of the sluggard craves and gets nothing, while the soul of the diligent is richly supplied." Paul urged Timothy regarding his ministry, "Do your best to present yourself to God as one approved" (2 Timothy 2:15). And Paul himself was a tireless, disciplined worker (see 1 Corinthians 9:26-27; Philippians 3:12-14).

However, the Scriptures also teach that success in any endeavor is under the sovereign control of God. As 1 Samuel 2:7 puts it, "The LORD makes poor and makes rich; he brings low and he exalts" (see also Psalm 75:6-7).

This explains why two students in the same major can both work diligently, yet one excels and gets top grades while the other barely gets above average. God may have given one more intellectual ability than the other or brought him into the world in a family that challenged and stimulated his intellectual growth. Whatever the cause, the ability to achieve or succeed ultimately comes from God. There is no such thing as the "self-made" person. From a human point of view, that person may appear to have succeeded by talent and tenacity and hard work. But who gave him those qualities? God.

To the Corinthians, Paul wrote, "Who sees anything different in you? What do you have that you did not receive? If then you received it, why do you boast as if you did not receive it?" (1 Corinthians 4:7). Maybe we should ask ourselves that question. What do we have that we did not receive from God? Nothing. Our intellect, our natural skills and talents, our health and energy, and our opportunities to succeed all come from God.

So you've got to wonder: Why are so many people so incredibly proud of themselves? Why are they so determined to show they've done better than others?

More important, why aren't they giving God any credit?

You see pride of achievement in all kinds of settings. Musicians showing off their Grammys. Valedictorians displaying their GPAs. Athletes waving around their trophies. Pastors one-upping each other over attendance records. One kid waving a test paper at another. Executives flaunting their company cars. The showing off can be the blatant "Look at me; I'm so great" stuff. It can be an offhand statement or even a "humblebrag" tweet that hides a boast inside a falsely modest statement.[1]

Unfortunately, you're just as likely to see it in Christians as non-Christians.

To me, one of the more obnoxious people is the blustery sort of person who lets everyone know that the secret to his success in school or business or ministry or whatever is his hard work. You expect that from an unbeliever, but when it comes from a Christian, it really is offensive.

And then there are the Christmas letters. You've seen them, right? Some of them are basically long lists of prideful boasts—from Mom's promotion at work to Dad's new book to Rachel's acceptance to an Ivy League school to little Daniel's Little League championship. Such letters basically shout, "Look at what a wonderful family we are. Look what we achieved. We just must be better than other people! You should envy us."

Now, am I saying we should never be happy about our blessings? Absolutely not! Should we never share our milestones with others? No again. I'm not even saying we should never admit to being happily "proud of ourselves."

I'm just saying we need to keep a close eye on how we think about our achievements. Are we falling into the sin of crediting only our own hard work and virtue? Are we using our achievements to subtly (or not so subtly) make other people feel like "less than" or losers? Most importantly, are we ignoring the ultimate Source of all good things in our lives?

Another aspect of the pride of achievement is the inordinate desire for recognition. All of us appreciate credit for a job well done. Who doesn't appreciate a little applause or a well-placed compliment? But what is our attitude when we do something well and *don't* receive recognition? Are we willing to labor in obscurity, doing our job "as to the Lord" (Colossians 3:23, KJV), or do we become disgruntled over the lack of recognition?

Two principles from Scripture can help us guard against a sinful desire for recognition. First, we should remember the words of Jesus in Luke 17:10, "So you also, when you have done all that you were commanded, say, 'We are unworthy servants; we have only done what was our duty.'" When we have done a job well or served faithfully over a long time, our attitude should be, "I have only done my duty."

Second, we should learn that all recognition, regardless of its immediate source, ultimately comes from God. It is God who puts down one person and lifts up another (see Psalm 75:6-7).

Putting these two principles together causes us to say, "All is of grace." I deserve nothing, and all I do receive, including recognition, comes only by the grace of God. Therefore, if I don't receive it, I will not fret.

## "YOU CAN'T TELL ME ANYTHING."

Before starting this book, I sent a proposed list of "acceptable" sins to about fifteen people in Christian ministry and asked them to add to the list any I had overlooked. From two who minister to students and young adults, I received a suggestion that I include the pride of an independent spirit. This spirit expresses itself primarily in two areas: resistance to authority, especially spiritual authority, and an unteachable attitude. Often these two attitudes go hand in hand. They reflect the pride of those who believe they know it all!

When I was young and single, I lived with two different families who had young children. I now remember with shame how I used to silently judge the way they were raising their kids. I was young and single with absolutely no experience in rearing children, yet I thought I knew more than they did.

In The Navigators' ministry, we often encounter a similar attitude among new and inexperienced staff. These folks are usually assigned to an intern role, serving under the direction of an experienced staff person. Yet they often come in with an attitude that they know more about the ministry than the person who is to train them.

The Bible is quite clear on the issue of submitting to authority. Of several Scriptures we could look at, the one that speaks most clearly to the subject is Hebrews 13:17: "Obey your leaders and submit to them, for they are keeping watch over your souls, as those who will have to give an account. Let them do this with joy and not with groaning, for that would be of no advantage to you."

The writer of Hebrews probably had in mind the spiritual authority of elders in a local church. However, the principle of submission and teachability applies in any situation where someone is under the tutelage or training of a more mature believer. And it is the pride of an independent spirit that makes us unteachable or unsubmissive, no matter our age.

I well remember the night I was first exposed to the teaching of Hebrews 13:17. At the time I was a fairly new naval officer, so I understood the concept of military authority. But the idea of submitting to a spiritual authority was a new and radical idea to me. I am grateful that God exposed me to this principle when He did. It so happened that the very next night I came in contact with The Navigators' ministry, which stresses one-to-one discipling and mentoring. Because of this new idea, I was teachable and responded readily to the challenges of being discipled by another person.

The Bible strongly teaches the value of a teachable attitude. Proverbs, in particular, has a lot to say about the subject. The first few chapters of Proverbs, for example, use the example of a father-son relationship to stress the value of being willing to learn from those more mature in faith (see, for example, Proverbs 3:1; 5:1; 7:1).

To give balance to this section, let me say that teachability doesn't mean becoming a clone or a carbon copy. It doesn't mean not thinking for yourself. It simply means being humble enough to admit you don't know everything and to listen to those who can help you grow.

Remember that all of us, young and old, are susceptible to the subtle sins of pride. So I urge you to pray over this chapter, asking God to bring to mind any of your prideful tendencies. As you do so, keep in mind God's promise from Isaiah 66:2:

> These are the ones I look on with favor
> those who are humble and contrite in spirit,
> and who tremble at my word. *(NIV)*

# YOUR TURN

REFLECT REFLECT "God opposes the proud." (James 4:6; 1 Peter 5:5)

## ENGAGE

1. This chapter lists four common varieties of sinful pride. Give examples of each from your own experience — either what you've seen in others or what you've battled in yourself.

   *① You see a girl in a little outfit and think how much better you are*
   *② arguments with others  ④ disobedience to*
   *③ recognition in sports               parents*

2. From this chapter as a whole, what are some effective ways to guard our hearts against sinful pride? Can you think of any others?

   *• Have a teachable spirit*
   *• Remember who you are in*
   *                    status*

3. Why does God hate sinful pride? How does it minimize His work in our lives? *God hates pride because it's what caused our sin. It took/takes away from His glory. It puts it all on us.*

## BRING IT TO GOD

Pray over this issue of pride, asking God to open your mind and heart to ways you've let pride infect your attitudes. If any come to mind, confess them to the Lord.

# CHAPTER 12

# SELFISH

Recently I learned that one of my heroes from a bygone era had some notable character flaws. One of his friends and admirers once wrote of him, "With all his glaring faults he was the greatest man I have known."

What were those glaring faults? Elsewhere, this same friend described him as heartless, domineering, and selfish.

I doubt my hero deliberately tried to be heartless, domineering, and selfish. Those qualities were simply blind spots for him. May God help us to deal with our own blind spots, including selfishness, as they occur in us.

In studying the sin of selfishness, it's helpful to start with the obvious truth that we were born with a selfish nature. Just spend an afternoon with preschoolers and you'll be totally convinced of that. How many times do you have to say, "Zach, share your toys with Austin" or "Bella, you mustn't grab toys from Eli like that"?

As those kids grow older, they learn that such obvious acts of selfishness are socially unacceptable, so they learn to disguise their selfish acts. But the problem doesn't go away. Even after we become Christians, our flesh still wars against the Spirit, and one of its expressions is selfishness.

Selfishness is a difficult sin to expose because it is so easy to see in someone else but so difficult to recognize in ourselves. In addition, there are degrees of selfishness as well as degrees of subtlety in expressing it. One person's selfishness may be obvious and in-your-face. Most of us, however, do care about what others think, so our expressions of selfishness will likely be more subtle.

Selfishness may take many forms in our lives, but for the purpose of looking at our "respectable" sins, I am going to address four areas of selfishness that I've often observed in believers.

## SELFISH ABOUT INTERESTS

Paul wrote in Philippians 2:4, "Let each of you look not only to his own interests, but also to the interests of others." Paul was undoubtedly referring to the concerns and needs of other people, but I am going to use the word *interests* in a narrower sense to mean subjects we are interested in.

At this stage of our lives, my wife and I are interested in our grandchildren. We like to talk about them and show pictures of them to our friends. The problem is that our friends like to do the same. If we're not sensitive to each other's interests when we're together, we may find ourselves waiting for our turn to share instead of enjoying what the other people show us.

That's just one example, of course. The same issue could arise in almost any field of interest. When involved with writing a book, I'm extremely interested in that project. So when other people ask me, "What are you writing about these days?" I find it easy to get carried away and spend too much time talking about my book. I have to remind myself that these people have interests of their own and give them the opportunity to talk about their interests.

Now, this form of selfishness may seem so harmless that you question why I include it in this chapter. At worst, it seems rude. But a glance at 2 Timothy 3:1-5 assures us that this kind of selfishness is indeed a sin. Paul provided a list of really ugly sins that will be characteristic of people in the "last days." And right there at the head of the list is "lovers of self."

"Lover of self" is a good description of a self-centered person. And a self-centered person cares little for the interests, needs, or desires of others. He is interested in only himself, and his self-centered conversation reflects that.

## SELFISH ABOUT TIME

Time is a precious commodity, and each of us has only a fixed amount in a day. Because most of us are very busy, it's easy to become selfish with our time. Whether we are men or women, young or old, we tend to guard our time for our own ends.

A student asks her roommate for help with an assignment, but the roommate is busy studying for an exam. Will she give up precious time to help her roommate, or will she either guard her time or help reluctantly?

What about the first student? Is she acting selfishly to ask her roommate for help when she knows the roommate is busy studying? We can be selfish in guarding our time, and we can also be selfish in unduly imposing on another person's time. In either case, we are thinking mainly about ourselves and our needs.

Selfishness with one's time will frequently be observed in the home. Usually every member of a household has his or her duties and responsibilities, and there is often a reluctance to go beyond these. "That's not my job," one person may say when asked to do something extra, with no sense of compassion toward one who seems overwhelmed. "I'll take care of that for you" seems to be a rare offer. Yet the Scriptures say that we are to "bear one another's burdens, and so fulfill the law of Christ" (Galatians 6:2). Going beyond our normal duties to help someone else is one way we can bear each other's burdens.

## SELFISH WITH MONEY

Surveys show that Americans, who live in one of the richest nations in all of history, give less than 2 percent of their income to charitable and religious causes. While we pride ourselves on our generosity following major disasters, the facts state that we Americans as a whole are selfish with our money and relatively indifferent to the physical and material needs of people less fortunate than us.

This is an especially crucial issue for believers. The apostle John wrote, "If anyone has the world's goods and sees his brother in need, yet closes his heart against him, how does God's love abide in him?" (1 John 3:17). This verse tells us that we are to cultivate hearts of compassion toward those in need and then put that compassion to work through our giving.

As has already been observed in an earlier chapter, every dollar we receive, even when earned by our work, is a gift from God. We are to be good stewards of that money and not spend all or most of it on ourselves. To do so is to be selfish with our money while ignoring the needs of others. (There is more on this subject in chapter 20.)

## THOUGHTLESSLY SELFISH

This trait may be expressed in several ways. Thoughtless or inconsiderate people rarely consider how their actions affect others. One person is always late and keeps others waiting. Another keeps her eyes glued on her phone and completely ignores other people in the room. Yet another costs a hardworking waitress in tips by lingering too long at a restaurant table or leaves a mess on the kitchen counter for someone else to clean up. Anytime we do not think about the impact of our actions on others, we are being selfish.

We can also be thoughtless about the feelings of others, treating them rudely or ignoring them altogether. I have often seen Christians treat wait staff or store clerks—or their own families—this way. And then there are people who just blurt out whatever they're thinking with no regard to whether their words may cause others to feel embarrassed or humiliated. Whenever we fail to consider the feelings of others, we are being selfish. And that's not okay!

The Bible makes it clear that we are to look not only to our own interests, but also to the interests of others. An *unselfish* person is always balancing his or her needs and concerns with the needs and concerns of others.

The greatest example of unselfishness is Jesus, who gave His very life for us. "Though he was rich," Paul explained, "yet for your sake he became poor, so that you by his poverty might become rich" (2 Corinthians 8:9). In seeking to become like Christ, we are called to put aside selfishness as well. In fact, we are to love the people around us as much as we love ourselves (see Matthew 22:39).

Living unselfishly comes at a cost. It costs time and money. It costs becoming interested in the interests and concerns of others and learning to be considerate of their needs and feelings. It costs sacrificing our built-in assumptions that we are the center of the universe. It may even cost us some self-esteem as we face the extent of our secret selfishness.

But here's the secret that followers of Christ have learned throughout the centuries: The more we are able, through the help of the Holy Spirit, to put self aside, the more love we'll have in our lives. Some of it may come from those around us. But more importantly, we'll draw closer to the One who is love in its purest form.

The love that is worth every sacrifice.

# YOUR TURN

"Love . . . does not insist on its own way." (1 Corinthians 13:4-5)

## ENGAGE

1. What are the four varieties of selfishness this chapter explores? Do any others come to mind? What varieties tempt you in your own life?

2. The author says that "there are degrees of selfishness as well as degrees of subtlety in expressing it." Can you give an example of subtle or hidden selfishness?

3. If we allow selfishness to take root in our lives, what consequences should we expect? Can you think of a time when you allowed this to happen? What did you experience as a result? How do you think other people felt about you?

## BRING IT TO GOD

Prayers can be selfish too! It's not wrong to pray for our own needs, but our prayers shouldn't be just about us. As a reminder of that truth, spend the next week praying *only* for the needs and concerns of others, not yourself.

# CHAPTER 13

# OUT OF CONTROL

"**A** man without self-control is like a city broken into and left without walls" (Proverbs 25:28).

In biblical times, a city's walls were its chief means of defense. If the walls were breached, it was vulnerable; an invading army could pour into the city and conquer it. In the same way, a person without self-control is vulnerable to all kinds of temptations.

Unfortunately, Solomon, who wrote Proverbs 25:28, is a sad but striking demonstration of this truth. Scripture records that Solomon had seven hundred wives and three hundred concubines, all from nations the Lord had specifically forbidden (see 1 Kings 11:1-3). Sure enough, these foreign women turned Solomon's heart away from God. In response, God divided Solomon's kingdom in the days of his son Rehoboam.

The Scriptures have a lot to say about self-control. Paul listed it as one expression of the fruit of the Spirit (see Galatians 5:22-23). He also mentioned the lack of it in his list of vices that will abound in the last days (see 2 Timothy 3:3). His instructions to Titus regarding his ministry in Crete included repeated instructions to teach self-control (see Titus 2:2,5,6) and a reminder that the same grace that brings salvation also trains us to live self-controlled lives (see Titus 2:11-12). And Peter's two letters urge us several times to be sober-minded, or self-controlled (see 1 Peter 1:13; 4:7; 5:8; 2 Peter 1:5-6).

Despite the scriptural teaching on self-control, I suspect this is one virtue that receives little *conscious* attention from most Christians.

We have cultural boundaries that tend to restrain us from obvious sins, but within those boundaries we pretty much live as we please. We seldom say no to our desires and emotions. And that's a shame, because it makes us vulnerable to other respectable sins. Not controlling our speech, for example, opens the door to "sins of the tongue" such as sarcasm, gossip, slander, and ridicule.

But what is self-control exactly? In simplest terms, it is saying no when we should say no. We handle our desires, cravings, impulses, emotions, and passions appropriately, with moderation in legitimate areas (say, watching TV) and complete restraint in those that are clearly sinful (such as Internet pornography).

Biblical self-control is different from willpower. Plenty of unbelievers exercise willpower in specific life areas while displaying little or no self-control in others. A model who sticks closely to a diet, for instance, may be unable to control her temper. But biblical self-control applies to every area of life and depends on the Holy Spirit for both motivation and power. We might say that self-control is not control *by* us, but rather control *of* us through the power of the Holy Spirit.

Though self-control is needed in all areas of life, in this chapter we will look at three areas where Christians often fail to exercise it.

## EATING AND DRINKING

I am not singling out those who have a weight problem. That may or may not be due to a lack of self-control. One of the most self-controlled men I have ever known struggled with weight all his adult life. And some people with hyped-up metabolisms can eat and drink whatever they please (at least for a time) with little regard for self-control.

What I am addressing is the tendency to continually give in to our desires for certain consumables. I think of a Christian acquaintance who used to drink twelve cans of soda every day. I also think of my own craving for ice cream. For years I would have a bowl at dinner and another at bedtime. God convicted me of my lack of self-control by showing me that this seemingly benign practice greatly weakened my self-control in other, more critical, areas. I learned that we cannot pick and choose the areas of life in which we will exercise self-control.

One of the ways we can exercise self-control is by removing or getting away from whatever tempts us. Now, instead of stocking ice cream in our freezer, my wife and I buy single servings for specific occasions. But even though I made that decision more than thirty years ago, the need for self-control remains. Recently I needed to mail a package at a contract post office that is located in an ice cream shop. On the way over, I began to fantasize about having a dish of ice cream. As I wrestled with that strong desire, I concluded this was a time when I needed to say no to myself just for the purpose of keeping that desire under control.

I'm not trying to lay a guilt trip on those who enjoy ice cream or soft drinks or even those who visit Starbucks every day. What I am addressing is our lack of self-control—a tendency to indulge our desires so that they control us instead of us controlling them.

## TEMPER

Some believers are known to be hot-tempered or to have a short fuse. Someone with a hot temper is prone to quick but intense bursts of anger that fade just as easily. Someone with a short fuse becomes angry or irritable easily. Many people have both. We will take up the sin of anger in a later chapter, but here I want to focus on the lack of control, which is also a sin.

Outbursts of temper are typically directed against anyone who displeases us, from a driver who cuts us off on the freeway to an umpire who makes a bad call. Unfortunately, family members are a frequent target.

The book of Proverbs warns repeatedly against sins of temper: Proverbs 16:32, for instance, says that "whoever is slow to anger is better than the mighty, and he who rules his spirit than he who takes a city." In the New Testament, James also admonished us to be "slow to anger" (1:19). Storing up such verses in our hearts (see Psalm 119:11) can help us exercise self-control over temper.

## PERSONAL FINANCES

Not too long ago, I heard a national radio speaker say that the average American household has a credit card debt of seven thousand dollars. The fact that this is the *average* debt indicates that Americans are spending beyond their means, indulging in desires for new clothes, the latest electronic or digital devices, expensive vacations, and the like. That this is a problem among Christians is attested by the fact that several Christian ministries are dedicated to helping Christians learn self-control in this area.

However, it is not just those in debt who fail to exercise self-control over their spending. Many affluent people, Christians included, simply indulge themselves in whatever their hearts desire. Even if we can easily afford to do this, it's not the way to gain the self-control that is the fruit of the Spirit. (We'll look at finances again in chapter 20.)

Food and drink, temper, and finances are not the only areas where we may need to learn self-control. Other areas include "screen time" (computers, TV), shopping, hobbies, and sports. In this age of sexual openness, there is a big need for self-control over our eyes and thought lives.

No doubt there are other areas that can easily lend themselves to a lack of self-control, so I encourage you to reflect on your own life. Are there desires, cravings, or emotions that may be out of control to some degree? As you seek to grow in this area of self-control, remember that it is a fruit of the Spirit. Only by God's enabling power will any of us make any progress in this area.

# YOUR TURN

"A man without self-control is like a city broken into and left without walls." (Proverbs 25:28)

## ENGAGE

1. What are some signals that the sin of self-control might be a problem—that our sinful desires are either starting to control us or have been controlling us? *when God does not become important to us + we put something above Him.*

2. Because biblical self-control is not a product of our natural willpower, what enables us to live self-controlled lives? (See Titus 2:11-12.) What does this insight mean to you personally?

   *the grace of God → because of my salvation, I have the ability to overcome.*

3. The author shares how a seemingly benign practice greatly weakened his self-control in more critical areas. In which areas are you tempted to use less self-control and give in to your desires? What would you say your "big three" self-control issues are?

   *Chocolate, games, and sports*

## BRING IT TO GOD

Say a prayer of thanks for the gift of the Holy Spirit, which is the key to avoiding the sin of insufficient self-control. If you have discerned the need for self-control in some area of your life, ask the Spirit for help.

# CHAPTER 14

# IMPATIENT AND IRRITABLE

A pastor friend of mine paid a visit to a couple who were greatly respected and loved in their church. The husband had terminal cancer and was nearing death.

"How are you doing spiritually?" the pastor asked.

With tears in her eyes, the wife responded, "We're doing well as far as the cancer is concerned. But what I can't handle is our sin. After all these years, and especially in this situation, you would think we wouldn't still hurt and wound each other, but we do."

This sad but true story illustrates an all-too-common reality: We tend to exhibit many respectable sins most freely at home. We can put on our "Christian face" outside the home, but with our families our true character often comes out. This is especially true in the two areas of sin we'll examine in this chapter: impatience and irritability.

## IMPATIENCE

These two traits are closely related, and both words can be defined in slightly different ways depending on the context. So for the purposes of this chapter, I am going to define impatience as a strong sense of annoyance at the (usually) unintentional faults and failures of others. This impatience is often expressed verbally in a way that tends to humiliate its target.

That word *unintentional* is key. We're not responding badly to people who want to bother us but rather to those who accidentally get in our way.

Because of my hearing disability, I can often *hear* my wife speaking to me but can't *understand* what she is saying, so I frequently ask her to repeat herself. This can be annoying, so she has had to get over her impatience with me when I do it.

My impatience with her usually concerns time. I like to live life with a time margin, starting out early enough to get to wherever I'm going in an unhurried fashion. My wife, on the other hand, has an incredible ability to be ready to go just in the nick of time. (How she times it this closely is a mystery to me.) So a standard scenario in our home is that I'll be ready to go but waiting on her. Will I bark out something like, "Why are you always late?" or stand there and tap my foot, communicating my impatience nonverbally? Or will I be patient with her, realizing that a harmonious relationship is more important than leaving the house at my prescribed time?

Temptations to show impatience crop up frequently at school, at church, at the workplace—anywhere people encounter each other. Here are a few more examples:

"How many times have I told you not to leave your shoes in the family room?" Parents often say something like this when kids are slow to respond to their training. Unfortunately, such impatient words rarely further the training efforts. They serve only to vent the parents' impatience and humiliate the child, who may respond in kind. Siblings in a family are often impatient with each other as well. Training children, by teaching and example, to be patient with others can be a challenge.

"Okay now, let's get moving!" Impatience is certainly not limited to a family context. It wants to emerge whenever something or someone gets in our way. Some Christians are notorious for being impatient drivers. We can become impatient over slow service at the bank or in a restaurant. I have to guard against impatience at a store checkout when I only want a pack of gum and the person ahead of me has a cart full of items. (The express lanes aren't always staffed.) And heaven help the infrequent traveler who is trying to figure out all the rules at the airport security checkpoint. ("*Everyone* knows to have your shoes off ahead of time!")

We all encounter daily frustrations like that and feel the temptations to lash out impatiently. All too often it's an action, not a temptation.

It's important to note, however, that neither my hearing disability nor my wife's close timing *causes* either of us to be impatient. They merely provide an opportunity for the flesh to assert itself. The actual cause of our impatience lies within our own hearts, in our own attitude of insisting that others around us conform to our expectations.

Paul stressed patience in several of his letters. He started his famous description of love in 1 Corinthians 13 with "love is patient" (verse 4). He included patience as a fruit of the Spirit (Galatians 5:22). In Ephesians 4:1-2, he urged us to live our lives with patience, and in Colossians 3:12, he said we are to "put on" patience. Paul clearly thought patience is a virtue to be cultivated, and he was writing under the Holy Spirit's guidance, not just expressing his opinion. Impatience is the opposite of this virtue, so it's reasonable to assume that impatience is a sin. Though it may be acceptable to us, it is not acceptable to God.

## IRRITABILITY

Impatience, as I have said, is a strong sense of annoyance or exasperation; it describes our reaction to being thwarted or bothered. Irritability, on the other hand, describes the *frequency* of our impatient response or the ease with which it can overtake us. The person who easily and frequently becomes impatient is an irritable person. Most of us become impatient at times, but an irritable person is impatient *most* of the time. This is the kind of person who makes others feel like they're walking on eggshells. He is no fun to be with, though family members or co-workers sometimes have no choice.

Are you often upset with someone or some circumstance? If so, you may need to learn to let some things go—or at least learn to bite your tongue. Proverbs 19:11, though addressing the topic of anger (our next chapter) says, "It is . . . glory to overlook an offense." And Peter wrote, "Love covers a multitude of sins" (1 Peter 4:8). We might say that if love covers a multitude of sins, how much more should it cover a multitude of irritations?

Now, suppose you are someone who is frequently the object of another person's impatience or irritability. Suppose you are often berated, criticized, or chewed out. How should you respond? It's all too tempting to respond in kind, triggering a war of words.[1] This approach is not only nonproductive, it is totally unbiblical.

Or you may be the type of person who doesn't respond verbally at all, but inwardly seethes and resents the person who has vented her impatience at you. This is also a sinful response on your part.

So what should you do? Biblically you have two options.

First, you can follow the example of Jesus, who, "when he was reviled, he did not revile in return; when he suffered, he did not threaten, but continued entrusting himself to him who judges justly" (1 Peter 2:23). Sometimes this is your only real option.

Second, you could choose to confront the person and point out examples of her impatience. This should be done only when you have resolved the issue in your own heart and can speak to the other person for her benefit, not just to make your own life more pleasant. If you can do this in a biblical manner and the person accepts what you say, you may be able to improve your relationship (see Matthew 18:15). However, if she becomes defensive or hostile, you need to revert to the first option.

Keeping your mouth shut and letting God judge isn't easy. It requires a strong conviction that He is in control and trust in His promise to work even this situation out for your good. But if you let Him, He can use even an impatient, irritable, annoying person to help you grow in the biblical virtues of patience and meekness.

## YOUR TURN

"I ... urge you to walk in a manner worthy of the calling to which you have been called, with all humility and gentleness, with patience." (Ephesians 4:1-2)

### ENGAGE

1. In your own words, define impatience and irritability. Give an example of each from your own life. What are your biggest temptations in this area?

   *impatience is getting edgy because something doesn't go your way. Irritability is a burst of anger because we are annoyed.*
   *★ Inward*

2. Do you agree with the author that circumstances or people's actions can never cause us to be impatient or irritable? Explain your answer. *Yes, it is our flesh and selfishness.*

3. What do you think are the real causes of impatience, irritability, and sinful anger? *Selfishness and not having love*

   Once we recognize them, what practical steps can we take to deal with them:

   - Proactively—before situations arise? *Pray*
   - Responsively—in the heat-of-the-moment situation? *Pray*
   - Retrospectively—once the Holy Spirit makes you aware that you've "blown it"? *Repent + go to the person*

## BRING IT TO GOD

This is the time to pray for patience in the daily annoyances and irritations of life. Ask the Holy Spirit for a spirit of calm and understanding in the face of all the daily annoyances of life. (Get specific about what tends to really annoy you now.)

# CHAPTER 15

# ANGRY

**W**hat is anger? You might say, "I can't define it, but I know it when I see it—especially if it's directed toward me."

My dictionary defines anger simply as a strong feeling of displeasure and usually of antagonism. I would add that it's often accompanied by sinful emotions, words, and actions that are hurtful to those who are the objects of our anger.

Robert Jones wrote that "anger is a universal problem, prevalent in every culture, experienced by every generation. No one is isolated from its presence or immune from its poison. It permeates each person and spoils our most intimate relationships. Anger is a given part of our fallen human fabric. Sadly, this is true in our Christian homes and churches."[1]

I would add that all too often our anger is directed toward those we should love most: the parents and siblings in our human families and brothers and sisters in our church families.

Anger is a huge and complex issue, and dealing with it extensively is beyond the purpose of this book. So I am going to focus on that aspect of anger that we unconsciously treat as "acceptable" sin. But first I want to take care of the issue of righteous anger.

Some people justify their anger as righteous. They feel they have a right, even a duty, to be angry. But how can we know if this is true?

First, true righteous anger arises from an accurate perception of true evil—that is, as a violation of God's moral law. It focuses on God and His will, not us and our will.

Second, righteous anger is always self-controlled. It never causes us to lose our temper or retaliate in some vengeful way.[2]

Though the Bible does give some examples of righteous anger, such as Jesus' cleansing of the temple (see Luke 19:45-48), they are few. The main focus of the Bible's teaching is sinful anger—our sinful reactions to other people's actions or words. That will be my focus too. This chapter is *not* about righteous anger—except perhaps the sinful anger we persist in calling righteous.

Also beyond the purpose of this book is anger that leads to verbal or physical abuse. I don't want to minimize the sin of abuse or the pain it causes. But such a situation calls for sound biblical and pastoral counseling, not a book on respectable sin. So I want to keep us focused on what we might call ordinary anger—anger that we sort of accept as part of our lives but is actually sinful in God's sight.

And let's be clear from the beginning: Nothing *causes* us to be angry.

Someone else's words or actions may become the occasion for our anger, but the real cause lies deep within us—usually our pride, or selfishness, or desire to control.

Say you agree to do something for a friend, then you forget. Your failure comes to light, and the friend gets angry. Why? Because your failure made him look bad in front of some of his friends. This is not to excuse your forgetfulness and the real fact that you put him in an awkward situation. But the cause of his anger was his pride, not your failure.

Or maybe you get mad because you don't get your way. We frequently see this in little kids, but people of all ages do it. Maybe you wanted to go to the mall with your friends but they wanted to play Frisbee at the park. They voted you down and you got angry. The cause is selfishness: "I want it my way."

It's not unusual to get angry as a response to someone else's anger. Say you get in some trouble at school for something somebody else did. The principal calls you into her office and really chews you out. She's so mad she won't even listen to your explanation; she just gives you detention. That makes you angry in return, but you can't exactly yell at the principal. Instead, you seethe inwardly with resentment. In fact, you're still mad when you show up for detention.

And get this: Your resentment is just as sinful as the principal's unreasonable anger.

I'm not trying to justify the principal's actions. I'm just trying to show that your anger belongs to you. The principal is responsible to God for her temper, but you're responsible to God for your resentment. You can *choose* how you respond to her sinful actions.

Consider Peter's words to slaves in the first-century churches, people who often served under cruel and unjust masters. According to much present-day thinking, their anger would be justified, but Peter wrote:

> Servants, be subject to your masters with all respect, not only to the good and gentle but also to the unjust. For this is a gracious thing, when, mindful of God, one endures sorrows while suffering unjustly. For what credit is it if, when you sin and are beaten for it, you endure? But if when you do good and suffer for it you endure, this is a gracious thing in the sight of God. (1 Peter 2:18-20)

Peter's instructions to slaves are a specific application of a broader scriptural principle: We are to respond to any unjust treatment as "mindful of God"—that is, with God's will and God's glory in mind. We should ask, *How would God have me respond in this situation? How can I best glorify Him by my response? Do I believe that this difficult situation or this unjust treatment is under the sovereign control of God and that in His infinite wisdom and goodness He is using these difficult circumstances to conform me more to the likeness of Christ?* (See Romans 8:28; Hebrews 12:4-11.)

I know that in the heat of an emotional moment, you're probably not going to ask questions like that. But it really is possible to get in the habit of thinking this way. Even if your immediate response is sinful anger, you can still reflect afterward on such questions and allow the Holy Spirit to dissolve your anger.

Now, there are probably exceptions to this that prove the rule, but it's pretty safe to say that all of us get angry from time to time. The issue is how we handle it. Some people tend to externalize their anger in strong, usually hurtful language. They may even yell. Others adopt subtler expressions such as zingers or sarcastic comments. And then there are those who tend to internalize their anger in the form of resentment.

And all of these expressions of anger are sin.

So what's the alternative? How should we handle our anger in a God-honoring way? I'd like to suggest a general outline:

- First, we have to *recognize* and *acknowledge* our anger and its sinfulness. We cannot deal with anger until we acknowledge its presence.
- Second, we need to *ask ourselves why* we are angry. Was it because of our pride or selfishness or some idol of the heart we are protecting?
- If so, third, we need to *repent* not only of our anger but also of the sinful attitude beneath it.
- Fourth, having to some extent dealt with the expression of our anger through recognition and repentance, we need to *change our attitude* toward the person or persons whose words or actions triggered our anger. Scriptures such as Ephesians 4:32 and Colossians 3:13 can help with this.
- Next, if we have expressed our anger outwardly, we need to *seek the forgiveness of the person we have wounded* by our anger.
- And finally, we need to hand the whole situation over to God.

This last item is especially important when we find ourselves the objects of someone else's anger or of unjust treatment by a boss, a parent, or anyone who treats us unfairly. To dissolve our sinful emotions, we must believe that God is absolutely sovereign in all the affairs of our lives (both the "good" and the "bad") and that all the words and actions of other people that tempt us to anger are somehow included in His wise and good purposes to make us more like Jesus. We must realize that any given situation that tempts us to anger can drive us either to sinful anger or to Christ.

## ANGER TOWARD GOD

I have encountered a number of Christians who are angry at God for some reason. Some of them think He has let them down in some way. Others believe God is actually against them. I sit here now looking at a letter that says, "I have felt so many times that He has slapped me in the face when I was really depending on Him." This person freely admitted to being angry at God because she had concluded that God was actually against her.

What are we to say to people who are desperately hurting and feel that God has let them down or is even against them? Is it okay to be angry toward God?

Most pop psychology would answer yes. "Just vent your feelings toward God." I've even read the statement, "It's okay to be angry at God. He's a big boy. He can handle it."

In my judgment, that is sheer blasphemy.

Let me make a statement loud and clear. It is *never* okay to be angry at God. Anger is a moral judgment, and in the case of God, it accuses Him of wrongdoing. It accuses God of sinning against us by neglecting us or in some way treating us unfairly. It often stems from the wrong assumption that God owes us a better deal in life than we are getting.

I think of a man who said as his mother was dying of cancer, "After all she's done for God, this is the thanks she gets." Never mind that Jesus suffered untold agony to pay for her sins so she would not spend eternity in hell. This man thought that God also owed her a better life on this earth.

I acknowledge that believers can and do have momentary flashes of anger at God. I have experienced this myself. We can't necessarily prevent them. But we can quickly recognize those flashes as the sins that they are and repent of them.

How, then, can we deal with our temptation to be angry at God? Must we just "stuff" our feelings and live in some degree of alienation from God? No, that is not the biblical solution.

We must begin, as I have said before (see chapter 8), with a well-grounded trust in the sovereignty, wisdom, and love of God. From there, we should bring our confusion and perplexity to God in a humble, trusting way—praying something like this: "God, I know that You love me, and I also know that Your ways are often beyond our understanding. I admit I am confused at this time because I do not see the evidence of Your love toward me. Help me, by the power of Your Spirit, to trust You and not give in to the temptation to be angry at You."[3]

Never forget that our God is a forgiving God. Even our anger toward Him, which I consider a grievous sin, was paid for by Christ in His death on the cross. So if you have anger in your heart toward God, I invite you—no, I urge you—to come to Him in repentance and experience the cleansing power of Christ's blood, shed on the cross for you.

I believe that many Christians live in denial about their anger. They consciously experience the flare-up of negative thoughts and emotions toward someone who has displeased them, but they do not identify this as anger, especially as sinful anger. Instead, they focus on the other person's wrongdoing and justify their own reaction. They do not see their sin. Consequently, their anger is "acceptable" to them and they sense no need to deal with it.

I pray that God will be pleased to use this chapter to help all of us, whether our anger is occasional or frequent, to recognize it as the sin it is and take appropriate steps to deal with it.

# YOUR TURN

 "I say to you that everyone who is angry with his brother will be liable to judgment; whoever insults his brother will be liable to the council; and whoever says, 'You fool!' will be liable to the hell of fire." (Matthew 5:22)

## ENGAGE

1. What form does your anger usually take? Is it direct and blustery, subtle and sarcastic, or internalized and seething—or none of the above? *depends on the situation, but normally either subtle or internalized.*

2. The chapter says that no one can make us be angry and that anger is always a choice. Do you agree or disagree?

   *Yes, I agree*

3. Outline the steps listed in this chapter for dealing with anger.

   *Recognize, Ask Why, Repent, Change my Attitude, Seek forgiveness, Hand it to God.*

4. Imagine that a good friend keeps justifying his or her sinful anger and refuses to face the deeper, causative issues. What might you say to him or her? *What she's doing is wrong and that God is not pleased or glorified.*

## BRING IT TO GOD

Write out your heart's prayer, asking God to help you, through His Holy Spirit, deal with anger proactively and positively this coming week.

Lord Jesus,

Please help me with my anger
and resentment. I know its wrong,
and I admit that I'm even angry
at you sometimes. Please forgive
me. I know you are not mortal
but immortal — you have never
done anything bad. You've always
worked your plan out for my good.

Thank you for that, and please
will me this week to glory
in Jesus Christ.

# CHAPTER 16

# IN THE WEEDS

Most of us tend to think of our anger as occurring in episodes. We get angry, and then we get over it. Maybe we apologize or maybe we don't, but somehow the person we're angry with gets over it and life goes on. The relationship has been scarred but not broken. It's not a great way to live with one another, but it's tolerable.

That seems to be the way far too many believers view the sin of anger. They've just come to accept it as part of life. But the Bible is not so tolerant of our anger. In fact, it basically tells us to get rid of anger (see Ephesians 4:31; Colossians 3:8).

If you take the time to look up these texts, you will see that in each of them, anger is associated with such ugly sins as bitterness, clamor, wrath, slander, malice, and obscene talk. It is also included in a similar list of despicable sins in 2 Corinthians 12:20. Clearly, anger does not keep good company. It often associates itself with what we would consider more serious sins and actually leads to some of them.

But what about the Scripture that says, "Be angry and do not sin; do not let the sun go down on your anger" (Ephesians 4:26)? Was Paul telling us it's okay to be angry or even commanding it? No. Paul was simply taking for granted that we will get angry and telling us how to handle it. Basically he was saying, "Don't hold on to your anger. Get over it quickly." That's why he added the clarifying statement, "Do not let the sun go down on your anger."

Have you ever heard the expression "Nip it in the bud"? That's what Paul was telling us to do with anger. Deal with it swiftly, and don't go to bed with it still in your heart. At best, anger is sin (with the rare exception of true righteous anger). At worst, it leads to even greater sins.

## WEEDS OF ANGER

In this chapter, we will look at some of the long-term results of anger—what I call "weeds of anger." I have deliberately chosen the word *weeds* because weeds are always something we want to get rid of. The weeds of anger are noxious, not benign. They can poison our minds and the minds of others around us.

What, then, are some of the noxious weeds that spring up from unresolved anger?

### RESENTMENT

Resentment is anger held in an iron grip. Most often it is internalized. It arises in the heart of a person who is ill-treated in some way but who does not feel able to do anything about it.

An employee may feel ill-treated by his boss but dares not react in an outwardly angry fashion, so he internalizes his anger as resentment. A wife may react similarly toward an abusive husband or a timid person toward an overbearing friend.

Resentment may be more difficult to deal with than outwardly expressed anger because resentful people often continue to nurse their wounds and dwell on their ill-treatment.

### BITTERNESS, ENMITY, HOSTILITY

Bitterness is resentment that has grown into a feeling of ongoing animosity. Whereas resentment may dissipate over time, bitterness continues to grow and fester, developing an even higher degree of ill will. It is usually the long-term reaction to real or perceived wrong when the initial anger is not dealt with.

An elder intervened in a situation regarding a teenage girl in his local church. The girl's father thought the elder had mishandled the situation. Instead of seeking to resolve the issue, he became angry and then bitter. In the words of the pastor, he was "eaten up with bitterness." The father said to the pastor, "I've forgiven him, but I don't want anything to do with him."

Quite obviously, he had not forgiven. True forgiveness results in a restored relationship, not continuing animosity. This man was consumed with bitterness, but in his self-righteousness he couldn't see it. All he could see was the perceived or actual wrong of the elder, which he continued to dwell on.

As this story illustrates, bitterness frequently occurs within a local church family. Someone is badly treated or at least she thinks she has been. Instead of seeking to resolve the issue, she allows her hurt to fester and over time becomes bitter. Or it may be that she did seek to resolve the issue and the other person did not respond. Perhaps she even went to someone on the pastoral staff who dismissed her complaint instead of listening carefully, intensifying her pain.

But regardless of the actual or perceived ill-treatment, bitterness is never a biblical option. We can be hurt and acknowledge that we have been hurt without becoming bitter.

Of course, bitterness can occur in any interpersonal relationship, but it's especially bitter when it grows among people who should love each other. The church family is one example. But bitterness may also occur in human families, among physical brothers and sisters. A son or daughter may feel that the parents are showing favoritism toward a sibling, and that perception may be accurate. But if the son or daughter is a Christian, he or she must not nurse that feeling until resentment becomes bitterness. For the person who wants to follow Christ, bitterness is never an option![1]

What about enmity and hostility? These are essentially synonymous and denote a higher level of ill will than does bitterness. Whereas bitterness may to some degree be marked by polite behavior, enmity or hostility is usually expressed openly. Often it takes the form of denigrating or even hateful speech toward or about the other person. And though bitterness may be harbored within one's own heart, enmity or hostility almost always spreads its poison outward to involve other people.

## GRUDGES

The word *grudge* (as in holding one) occurs five times in the Bible: Genesis 27:41; 50:15; Leviticus 19:18; Psalm 55:3; Mark 6:19. In the Genesis texts, the English Standard Version translates the Hebrew word as "hate"—showing us just how much animosity and ill will are implied by the word. In all five occurrences, the word is associated with taking revenge on the object of the grudge.

For example, Esau *hated and held a grudge against* Jacob and planned to kill him (see Genesis 27:41).

Joseph's brothers were afraid he would *hate or hold a grudge against* them and pay them back for all the evil they had done to him (see Genesis 50:15).

In the New Testament, Herodias *had a grudge against and hated* John the Baptist and wanted to put him to death (see Mark 6:19).

Today we probably wouldn't associate holding a grudge with plans to kill someone, though people will sometimes plot some form of revenge toward the person they hold a grudge against. They don't usually execute those plans, but they get a perverse enjoyment out of going over them in their minds. This can be true even among Christians. That is why Paul found it necessary to write the exhortation of Romans 12:19-21: "Beloved, never avenge yourselves, but leave it to the wrath of God, for it is written, 'Vengeance is mine, I will repay, says the Lord.' To the contrary, 'if your enemy is hungry, feed him; if he is thirsty, give him something to drink; for by so doing you will heap burning coals on his head.' Do not be overcome by evil, but overcome evil with good."

## STRIFE

Strife describes open conflict or turmoil between parties, usually between opposing groups. That's why we speak of "church fights" or "family feuds." It almost always goes beyond the bounds of "respectable" sins, and it certainly isn't subtle, but I include it because it often occurs between self-righteous Christians who never consider the possibility that their own attitudes or heated words contribute to the strife. In their minds, it is always the other party who is in the wrong and is causing the problems.

# HOW TO NIP IT IN THE BUD

The previous descriptions of these noxious "weeds of anger" are not intended to be definitive, nor do I mean to draw a sharp distinction between them. Terminology here is not important. What I want us to see is that the anger we hold on to is not only sinful, but spiritually dangerous.

If you will scan back over these weeds, you'll see the escalation of ill will and dissension. Anger is never static. If it is not dealt with, it will grow into bitterness, hostility, revenge-minded grudges, and outright strife. No wonder that Paul said, "Do not let the sun go down on your anger."

How, then, can we nip our anger in the bud so that it does not begin to sprout these noxious weeds? How can we make sure the sun does not go down on it? Let me give three basic directions.

### #1: REMEMBER WHO'S IN CHARGE.

All right, here comes that sovereignty thing again! I keep repeating it because it's absolutely crucial to keep in mind. God doesn't cause people to sin against us, but He does allow it, and always for a purpose.

After Joseph's brothers attacked him and sold him into slavery—a truly terrible way to treat their little sibling—he did not become bitter. Instead he told his brothers, "It was not you who sent me here, but God" (Genesis 45:8). Granted, he said those words after he had been promoted to a high office in Egypt, but they were true from the day he was tied up and slung over that camel. And during the years when he was a slave and then a prisoner for a crime he didn't commit, the biblical narrative never suggests Joseph became bitter. Instead it tells us that he did his work well and was so well regarded that both his owner and the keeper of the prison assigned him major responsibilities.

I too have found that a firm belief in God's sovereignty is my first defense against the temptation to hold on to anger. If I want to deal with the temptation decisively, I remind myself that whatever happened to trigger my initial response of anger is under God's active control and that God can use even another person's sin to my benefit. As Joseph told his brothers, "As for you, you meant evil against me, but God meant it for good" (Genesis 50:20).

What good does God have in mind? Often it's an opportunity to grow in Christlikeness. Sometimes I learn later that He's been preparing me for greater usefulness. Sometimes I just don't know. But it still makes a huge difference to know that even when someone else wrongs me, God intends good. Keeping God's sovereignty on my mind is my first step to keep anger from growing into weeds.

## #2: KEEP ON LOVING.

The book of 1 Peter is a letter urging its readers to pursue holiness even in the face of tough times. But also, again and again, it emphasizes the importance of love toward our fellow believers. "Above all," Peter wrote, "keep loving one another earnestly, since love covers a multitude of sins" (4:8).

Love makes it possible to maintain relationships even when others sin against us. If someone snubs us or inconveniences us or embarrasses us, love helps us overlook it. Remember, we can choose how we react to the real or perceived wrong actions of other people, and love is an incredibly powerful choice.

The apostle Paul echoed Peter's words when he wrote that love "is not easily angered" (1 Corinthians 13:5, NIV). That's a statement we all need to ponder. Are you easily angered? Can just a little sarcastic remark by someone almost ruin your day, or can you, out of love for the person who made the remark, shrug it off or "cover" it?

Everyone knows that the old rhyme "Sticks and stones may break my bones, but words can never hurt me" simply isn't true. Sinful words do hurt, especially if they come from someone close to us. But we can still choose whether those words will make us angry. We can absorb the hurt without entertaining anger. But to do that, we must really love the other person.

Paul also told us that love "keeps no record of wrongs" (1 Corinthians 13:5, NIV). Do you tend to file away in your mind wrongs done to you? This is a sure road to bitterness. The statement "I can forgive, but I can't forget" simply isn't true. If you keep rehearsing in your mind old hurts that occurred months or maybe even years ago, you haven't forgiven. You are simply feeding your bitterness.

To keep no record of wrongs means we cease to bring them up to ourselves or to another party. It does not mean we magically erase the hurt from our memories. We can't do that. But we can avoid actively calling it up and feeding on it. And if it comes to our minds involuntarily, perhaps triggered by another incident, we can immediately dismiss it. We can refuse to give it a foothold in our conscious thinking.

## #3: LEARN TO FORGIVE (AS GOD HAS FORGIVEN YOU).

The Scripture that helps me most to practice forgiveness in the face of forgiveness is the parable of the unforgiving servant (see Matthew 18:21-35). Jesus told that story in response to Peter's question, "How often will my brother sin against me, and I forgive him?" But Jesus didn't give him a number. Not exactly. Instead, He told a parable that cuts to the heart of how we can forgive.

The story is about a king's servant who owed his master ten thousand talents. That's a huge sum of money, the equivalent of two hundred thousand years of wages for the typical laborer—six to eight billion dollars in our present-day labor market. Jesus was clearly using hyperbole (extravagant exaggeration) to make His point, because there was no way a mere servant could have accumulated such a huge debt. But we'll see shortly why Jesus used such an immense sum of money.

The servant begged for time to repay what he owed. This was purely wishful thinking on the servant's part. There was no way he could repay that huge debt. So the king took pity on him and forgave the debt entirely.

Then this servant went and found a fellow servant who owed him a hundred denarii—about one-third of a year's wages or, by today's reckoning, about ten to fifteen thousand dollars. This second servant also pleaded for time to repay. But the servant who had just been forgiven of more than six billion dollars refused and had his fellow servant thrown in jail.

The message of the parable turns on the vast difference between the two debts. One was more than six billion dollars. One was only ten to fifteen thousand dollars, not an insignificant sum, but nothing in comparison to six billion.

Now, the first sum of money represents our moral and spiritual debt to God. Though in the master-servant world of Jesus' day, the amount would be preposterous, it's a pretty accurate representation of what we owe God. So we all are represented by the first servant who owed ten thousand talents. Because regardless of how moral and spiritual we have been, the debt of our sin is utterly unpayable.

But let's go back to the parable. What happened to the billions of dollars the first servant owed? Could the king just walk away and forget it? Were there no financial consequences to him? No, it's not that easy. The moment the king forgave the debt, his net worth was reduced by six to eight billion dollars. Forgiving the servant's debt cost the king tremendously.

In the same manner, it cost God to forgive us. It cost Him the death of His Son. No price can be put on that death, but God paid it so He could forgive each of us of the enormous spiritual debt we owed to Him.

The message should be clear. The moral debt of wrongdoing, of sinful words and acts against us, is virtually nothing compared to our debt to God.

I'm not minimizing the seriousness of hurts or damages you may have experienced. In the parable, ten to fifteen thousand dollars was a lot more than coffee-break money at work. It was a third of a year's wages. And the wrongs you have suffered may be much more than an occasional snub or word of gossip about you. They may well have caused you quite a bit of pain. But compared to the damage each of us has done to God's glory, it's a small amount.

The basis of our forgiveness for one another, then, is the enormity of God's forgiveness for us. Until we acknowledge that we are the ten-thousand-talent debtor to God, we will struggle with forgiving people who have wronged us in significant ways or people who continue to wrong us. But once we embrace the reality that we truly are such debtors to God because of our *continual* sin against Him, the whole picture changes. When someone wrongs us or even hurts us profoundly, we can still say, "God, that was a terrible wrong against me, but I am the ten-thousand-talent debtor. That other person's sin against me was nothing compared to my sin against you. And because You have forgiven me, I choose to forgive that person as well."

I don't want to imply that praying in such a way, even when done sincerely, will cause our anger to immediately disappear. The flesh doesn't give up that easily. But the attitude expressed in such a prayer does give us a weapon for putting our anger to death.

You might even say it's the perfect "weed eater" for our anger.

## YOUR TURN

"Let all bitterness and wrath and anger and clamor and slander be put away from you, along with all malice." (Ephesians 4:31)

### ENGAGE

1. Why is it so important to nip anger in the bud? What can happen if you don't?

   *If we don't, it will get bigger & bigger.*

2. If ongoing anger is painful, why do you think people insist on holding on to it in the form of resentment, bitterness, grudges, and strife?

   *They don't want to forgive*

3. How is it practically possible to choose an honest, loving response when you have been deeply hurt or offended? What is necessary for that to happen?

   *Because of christ — forgiveness.*

4. Looking back on your life, what has been the hardest wrong for you to forgive? Have you been able to put it behind you yet? Why or why not?

   *Probably Julia... yes — because I realized that, Christ forgave me, so I should forgive those involved.*

### BRING IT TO GOD

Practice the prayer of the ten-thousand-talent debtor, filling in a real person's name if appropriate: "God, _____'s sin against me was nothing compared to my sin against You. And because You have forgiven me, I choose to forgive _____ as well."

# CHAPTER 17

# JUDGMENTAL

The sin of judgmentalism is one of the most subtle of our "respectable" sins because it is often practiced under the guise of standing up for what is right. It's obvious that within our conservative evangelical circles there are multiple opinions about everything from what we believe to how we act to what our politics are, and most of us assume our opinions are correct. That's where judgmentalism begins, when we equate our opinions with truth.

Of course, judgmentalism is not limited to conservative evangelicals. It permeates our society and occurs on either side of the cultural divide. Animal rights activists who burn medical research clinics and extreme environmentalists who vandalize ski slopes are acting out their judgmentalism. The person who says, "Jesus wouldn't drive an SUV" is judgmental, not because Jesus *would* drive an SUV (that's not the point) but because the person has made a dogmatic and judgmental statement based purely on personal opinion.

I grew up in the middle of the twentieth century, when people dressed up to go to church. Men wore jackets and ties—usually suits and ties—and women wore dresses. That's just the way it was. Then, sometime in the 1970s, men started showing up at church wearing casual slacks and open-collared shirts, and women began to wear pants. (Jeans weren't even on the radar for church back then, although that would come.)

For several years, I was judgmental toward this more casual style of dress. *Don't they have any reverence for God?* I wondered.

I was wrong.

There is nothing in the Bible that tells us what we ought to wear to church. And reverence for God, I finally concluded, is not a matter of dress, but a matter of the heart. Jesus said that true worshippers are those who worship the Father in spirit and truth (see John 4:23). Casual clothing might possibly reflect a casual attitude toward God, but I cannot look at a casually dressed person and know that's his or her attitude. Therefore, I should avoid ascribing an attitude of irreverence based purely on what a person is wearing.

I also grew up in the era of grand old hymns sung to the accompaniment of piano and organ. To me, that was the way worship should be. Then praise music began to replace the hymns I loved. Drums and guitars appeared on worship platforms. And again I was judgmental. *How can people worship God with those instruments?* It took me a while to remember that the New Testament churches had neither pianos nor organs, yet they managed to worship in "psalms and hymns and spiritual songs" (Colossians 3:16).

I still have a preference for church music sung as we did when I was younger, but it's just that—a preference, not a Bible-based conviction. The same is true for those who love contemporary music and think the old hymns and organ music sound stuffy and boring. That's a preference too, nothing to be judgmental about.

Some issues involve more than simple preference, of course. Some are matters of conviction. I remember a polite but firm letter I received from a woman who read something I wrote about drinking alcohol. After much thought and study, I'd concluded that in most instances the Bible teaches temperance, not abstinence. I had done that study because I found myself being judgmental when I would see Christians having a glass of wine at a restaurant. But the woman who wrote in was convinced I was selling out a foundation stone of Christian morals.

Please don't get me wrong. I'm not advocating alcohol use. In fact, I believe that the widespread abuse of alcohol in our society makes a good case for abstinence. But this chapter is about judgmentalism, and I'm just giving some first-person examples of how easy it is to become judgmental over issues the Bible does not address with the clarity we would like—or address at all.

The apostle Paul faced this problem head-on in Romans 14. The church there was divided over the issue of what Christians should eat. Some people ate only vegetables; others thought it was fine to eat anything (presumably meat). The vegetarians thought they had the moral high ground and looked down their religious noses at those who ate anything. The "eat anything" crowd thought they had superior knowledge. They *knew* that what they ate made no difference to God if it was received with thanksgiving (see 1 Timothy 4:4). So they were judgmental in a different way.

Sounds familiar, doesn't it? Judgmentalism can be a two-way street. But judgmentalism is also a sin, no matter which side of an issue we're on. It's just so tempting to disdain anyone whose opinions are different from ours, then hide our judgmentalism under the cloak of Christian convictions.

Paul's response to the situation in Rome was, "Stop judging one another regardless of which position you take." And then he added, "Who are you to pass judgment on the servant of another? It is before his own master that he stands or falls. And he will be upheld, for the Lord is able to make Him stand" (Romans 14:4).

Basically Paul was saying, "Stop trying to pretend you're completely blameless in your interactions with fellow believers in Christ. God is the judge, not you."

Playing God—that's what we're doing when we judge others. We're claiming a role God has reserved for Himself. And that's sin.

Don't misunderstand me. I'm not saying we should never make judgments regarding the practices and beliefs of others. Scripture clearly condemns some actions, such as those described in Romans 1:24-32, Galatians 5:19-21, and 2 Timothy 3:1-5. When we judge them as sin, we are simply agreeing with the Word of God.

I believe we also need to make judgments concerning matters of doctrine, or Christian belief. Certain teachings are essential to biblical faith and need to be defended. But even here, we need to be careful. Because sound doctrine is important to me, I confess I have slipped into judgmentalism. I disagree so strongly with what some evangelicals are teaching that unfortunately I have sometimes demonized them. And though I believe I was right in my position, my judgmental attitude was sinful.

The point is, we can still sin even when we judge according to Scripture and right doctrine. We sin if we judge harshly or with an attitude of self-righteousness. We sin if we condemn the obvious sins of others without acknowledging that we, too, are sinners before God. One of the major objectives of this book is to help us stop doing that.

## A CRITICAL SPIRIT

Most of us can slip into the sin of judgmentalism from time to time, but some of us practice it continually. These people have what I call a critical spirit. They look for and find fault with everyone and everything. Regardless of the topic of conversation—whether it's a person, a church, a preference, or an activity—they end up speaking in a disparaging manner. I'm not writing about hypothetical people. I've been with some of them, and they are not pleasant to be around.

In earlier chapters, I have mentioned that some of our acceptable sins—selfishness, impatience, and anger—are often expressed more freely at home than in public, especially the Christian public. This is true of a critical spirit. Husbands and wives, parents and children, even siblings often hurt each other with this ongoing form of judgmentalism.

A friend of mine tells of being raised in an upper-middle-class Christian home where the father displayed this critical spirit toward his middle child. He was always putting her down "for her own good," and the constant barrage of criticism gradually wore her down. The more he criticized her posture, the more she slumped. The more he pointed out her lack of eye contact, the more she stared at the floor.

Eventually that father's judgment of his daughter became a self-fulfilling prophecy. She felt her father's pattern of criticism as rejection and came to see herself as a reject. As an adult, she clung to anyone who offered her acceptance, and her "friends" soon learned how to take advantage of her need.

On his deathbed, the father realized his sinfulness and tearfully repented of his critical spirit toward his daughter. But it was too late. By then she was a crack addict.

This is an extreme example, true, but it gives an idea of how destructive this sin can be. It is often said that it takes seven compliments to undo the effects of one criticism. So let's examine ourselves or, better yet, subject ourselves to the examination of others. Do we tend to find fault with others, especially members of our own family or members of our own church? Is our judgment harsh or unrelenting? If there's even a slight chance this might be true, we need do whatever is necessary to put this highly destructive sin to death.

As I wrap up this chapter, I'm aware that some of my dearest friends may disagree with some things I've said in this chapter. You may disagree too, and I'm okay with that. I respect your right to read the Bible, think through the issues, and come to your own conclusions.

I'd like to be like Paul, who took a similar position regarding the divisive issues in Rome. He did not try to change anyone's convictions regarding what they ate. Instead, he said, "Each one should be fully convinced in his own mind" (Romans 14:5).

Such a statement makes many of us uncomfortable. We don't like ambiguity in issues of Christian practice. It's difficult for us to accept that one person's opinion can be different from ours and both of us be accepted by God. But that is the position Paul took. And if we will take him seriously and hold our convictions with humility, we'll find it easier to resist the subtle — or not so subtle! — sin of judgmentalism.

## YOUR TURN

"There is only one lawgiver and judge, he who is able to save and to destroy. But who are you to judge your neighbor?" (James 4:12)

### ENGAGE

1. Describe some examples of judgmentalism you've seen (or felt!) in your church, at school, in your community, or on the Internet. What kind of person or issue most tempts you to be judgmental or hypercritical? *What I wear, how I act, my family → homeschool / overly conservative or extreme liberalism*

2. Judgmentalism begins, writes the author, when "we equate our opinions with truth." What's the difference between a preference for something and a Bible-based conviction? What can happen when we elevate personal convictions to the level of biblical truth—even when the Bible is not clear on that particular issue? *A preference is based solely upon personality or how you've been raised. Bible-based conviction is a truth you've gotten from the Bible → We become proud.*

3. How does the author distinguish between "making judgments" and "being judgmental"? How is the perspective of Bible-based confrontation different from much of our society's emphasis on "tolerance"? *• Bible-based confrontation is something specific that is clearly sinful, so it needs to be dealt with. Tolerance has to do with rights.*

### BRING IT TO GOD

Meditate on your answer to the first question above. Take your personal judgment issues to the Lord in prayer. Confess any lapses into a judgmental spirit and pray for a sweet and discerning spirit instead.

# CHAPTER 18

# COMPETITIVE

I recently learned that a writer friend of mine receives frequent requests for speaking engagements all over the world. *But I have written as many books as she has,* I thought. *Why don't I receive those kinds of invitations?*

And here's the funny thing. I didn't even *want* to go overseas. I just wanted to have the same kind of recognition.

Score one for envy. I moved past it quickly, but I have to admit I felt the twinge.

Envy is one of a group of actions and attitudes I call competitive sins. They all involve our reactions to those we perceive as somehow threatening our position or possessions.

Envy in particular is the painful awareness of an advantage enjoyed by someone else. Sometimes we want that same advantage, and sometimes we just resent that the other person has something we don't.

Usually, there are two conditions that tempt us to envy: We envy those we most identify with, and we envy in them the areas we value most. My friend fits both these descriptions. She and I work in the same field of teaching and writing, which I value. And we both enjoy a similar standing in that field, with some recognition but not exactly a "high profile" career. I see her as a peer, which makes me more likely to envy her.

I am never tempted to envy musicians or artists or highly successful business and professional people. Their talents and expertise are completely different from mine, so I don't tend to compare myself with them. And even in my field of teaching and writing, many are so much more gifted than me that envy is not an issue.

Consider a young baseball player in the minor leagues, hoping to someday make it to the majors. He doesn't envy the major league stars. They are out of his league. But he might envy the guy in the dugout next to him, especially if he believes the other player is receiving favor from the team manager.

Do you see my point? The reason envy tempts us in such situations is that there are enough similarities that the differences strike us more painfully. In the same way, the parents of a "problem child" may envy other parents whose children aren't in trouble. Elementary kids may envy the classmate who gets to take the hamster home. The possibilities are endless.

But when we are tempted to envy, we should realize that envy, though it may be a subtle and seemingly minor sin to us, is listed among the vile sins that Paul catalogued in Romans 1:29 and Galatians 5:21. It's right up there with drunkenness and murder!

## JEALOUSY

*Jealousy* and *envy* are sometimes used interchangeably, but there is a subtle distinction that can help us see the sinfulness of our hearts. Envy is resent of a peer who has an advantage over us. But jealousy is intolerance of rivalry.

Jealousy is not always a sin. For instance, God declares Himself to be a jealous God who will not tolerate the worship of anyone or anything other than Himself (see Exodus 20:5). But sinful jealousy occurs when we fear someone will become equal to or even superior to us.

The classic example of this in the Bible is found in King Saul's relationship with David. After young David slew Goliath, the women of Israel sang, "Saul has struck down his thousands, and David his ten thousands" (1 Samuel 18:7). After that, Saul regarded David as a rival and was jealous of him.

We, too, can be jealous if we have been blessed by God in some area of life or ministry and then someone comes along whose performance or results are superior to ours. Say, for instance, that a high-school senior named Angela has finally been named first-chair trumpet in her school band. Then a freshman named Micah appears, and Micah plays the trumpet very well. Within months, the new kid is threatening Angela's first-chair status—and she is jealous.

Situations like this happen all the time, in many different walks of life. So how can we deal with the temptation to envy others or to become jealous of them?

What helps me most is to bring God into the picture. I have to  remind myself that He is the One who gives us all our talents, abilities, and spiritual gifts.

It's obvious as we look around that some are better trumpeters than others. Some write better or sing better. Some are more adept at working with their hands. There also seems to be a widespread diversity in God's blessing on those gifts. It is God who puts down one and exalts another (see Psalm 75:7). So being envious or jealous of another person is either eliminating God from the picture or else accusing Him of being unfair.

Another way to combat sinful envy or jealousy, especially when it comes to other believers, is to remember that we are all "one body in Christ, and individually members one of another," so we should "outdo one another in showing honor" (Romans 12:5,10). Instead of being envious of those who have some advantage over us or jealous of those who may be overtaking us in some way, we should honor and applaud them as members of the same body.

Finally, it helps to remember that spending emotional energy on envy or jealousy can blind us to our place in God's plan. God has an assignment for each of us. Some assignments may garner more human recognition than others, but all are important.

## COMPETITIVENESS

Closely allied with envy and jealousy is the competitive spirit: the strong urge to always win or be the top person in whatever our field of endeavor. This begins at an early age. Young children can throw a fit when they don't win at tic-tac-toe! But I've seen adult Christians completely lose it when a golf game didn't go their way or their kid's soccer team came in last.

I'm not talking here about friendly competition, which can be healthy. A little competition can motivate us to push ourselves, learn new skills, and handle losing graciously. It can promote excellence not just in sports, but at science fairs and spelling bees and battles of the bands.

The competitive spirit is different. It's basically an expression of selfishness, the desire to build ourselves up at someone else's expense. It definitely is not compatible with loving our neighbor as ourselves.

I realize I'm questioning a sacred cow in our culture, which has elevated the competitive spirit to a virtue. We teach children directly and by example that "killing the competition" is the way to get ahead in the world. I question, however, whether a competitive spirit is a Christian virtue.

Rather than blessing competitiveness, the Bible tells us, "Do your best to present yourself to God as . . . a worker who has no need to be ashamed" (2 Timothy 2:15). Colossians 3:23 says we are to "work heartily, as for the Lord." And of course our efforts should be motivated by a desire to glorify God, not win recognition for ourselves. The recognition may come, but it should not be our motivation.

Therefore, Angela the trumpeter should concentrate on doing her best to play music in a God-honoring way. If her best wins her first chair, she should not be proud but grateful to God for giving her the ability. If it loses her the first-chair position, she will still have the satisfaction of playing as well as she could.

Someone may argue that Paul endorsed the competitive spirit in 1 Corinthians 9:24: "Do you not know that in a race all the runners run, but only one receives the prize? So run that you may obtain it." But the analogy breaks down at the point of the prize. In a race, only one runner wins and receives the prize. But in the Christian life, we all may receive the prize. Paul was not urging us to compete with one another. He was just telling us to run with the intensity of a track star, focusing hard on the finish line.

You can see now that there is a close relationship between envy, jealousy, and competitiveness. We tend to envy a peer who enjoys an advantage in an area we value highly. We become jealous of a person who is overtaking us. And both of these attitudes involve a competitive spirit that says, "I must always be number one." It's just another way of proclaiming, "It's all about me"—a sinful contradiction of the biblical message.

## CONTROLLING

There is one more subtle sin that I believe fits in this group: seeking to control others to get what we want.

I once asked a pastor about the source of friction between a couple in his church. He replied without hesitation: "She wants to control everything." I understand what he was talking about because I've seen it so many times, and not just in marriage and certainly not just with women. Control is an equal-opportunity sin. You see it in children on the playground, in the cafeteria at school, in offices and churches and nursing homes. It happens when one person is determined to make all the decisions and get his or her way, no matter what.

Controllers use a variety of methods. Some simply dominate others by sheer force of willpower and personality. Some pout or sulk when their decisions are questioned or their desires are thwarted. Some argue all the time. Still others use sweet talk and flattery or resort to character assassination. And manipulation is a favorite tactic.

The truth is, most controllers will use any means necessary to get what they want. Instead of submitting to each other the way the Bible urges (see Ephesians 5:21), they make sure their wishes prevail. The difficulty in addressing this sin is that controllers are sometimes the last ones to recognize this tendency in their lives. In their minds, they're just making sure things are done right.

Because we all have the flesh waging its guerrilla warfare in us, we still have blind spots of sin in our lives. We may need both the convicting power of the Holy Spirit and the help of other Christians to help us see our subtle sins. So I urge you to ask God to help you see tendencies toward controlling others (or envy, jealousy, competitiveness, or any other subtle or not-so-subtle sin).

Ask those closest to you to give you honest feedback. If you are a controlling person, you may find they are reluctant to do that because of your past behavior. So you must demonstrate true humility in asking them, maybe more than once, and then listen. Instead of becoming defensive—or using the other people's words against them—take their advice to God to help you.

I once confronted a controller-type person in our ministry about this tendency in his life. Actually, I was the third person to do so. But instead of hearing me, he got upset and severed our relationship. I have not seen him in some years. But the last I heard, he still had the same problem. He refused to face his sin.

Don't be like that. Don't go through life harboring envy or jealousy or always having to win or get your way. Remember, "God opposes the proud but gives grace to the humble." Don't place yourself in the position of being opposed by God.

# YOUR TURN

 "The works of the flesh are evident: ... jealousy, fits of anger, rivalries, dissensions, divisions, envy." (Galatians 5:19-21)

## ENGAGE

1. Read Romans 1:29 and Galatians 5:19-21. Why do you think the competitive sins are included in these lists of really bad sins? Why are they so harmful?

2. Do you think that simply feeling envy, jealousy, competitiveness, or control is sinful in itself? Are these actual choices? If not, at what point do they become choices—and sin? *Simply feeling*

*They are actual choices*

3. What control tactics have you seen people around you use? Which ones do you tend to use to get your own way?

*argue, pout, manipulation*
*→ argue or flattery*

4. If God were to underline any parts of this chapter for you, what might He mark? Why? *jealousy — I always seek to be the best at everything.*

## BRING IT TO GOD

Ask God to point out areas in your life where you might be prone to the competitive sins. Ask for the Spirit's help in accepting your place in God's plan and using your unique giftedness for God's glory.

# CHAPTER 19

# VERBAL

It's happened to me over and over. Someone comes up to me at a social gathering and asks what I'm working on. I answer that it's a book about sins that Christians often tolerate. "Oh," the other person says, "you mean like gossip."

Apparently, gossip is a biggie in Christian circles, but it's far from the only "talking sin." Any speech that tears down another person—someone we are talking about or someone we are talking to—is sinful speech. And the Bible is full of warnings against that. Proverbs alone contains about sixty. Jesus warned that we will give account for every careless word we speak (see Matthew 12:36). And then there is that well-known passage in James 3 that speaks of how powerful and destructive the human tongue can be. James said it's like a deadly poison or a small fire that sets a forest ablaze!

The Scripture that has helped me most to deal with my own talking sins, however, is Ephesians 4:29: "Let no corrupting talk come out of your mouths, but only such as is good for building up, as fits the occasion, that it may give grace to those who hear." This verse is an application of Paul's "put off/put on" principle described in Ephesians 4:22-24. We are to put off the sinful traits of the old self and put on the gracious traits of the new self created in Christ. In this case, we're putting off negative speech and putting on positive, grace-filled speech.

Note Paul's absolute prohibition: *No* corrupting talk. This means *no* gossip, *no* sarcasm, *no* critical speech, *no* harsh words. All forms of speech that could tear down others must be banished from our speech, including that Christian biggie, gossip.

Gossip involves spreading personal "news" about someone else. Even if the information is true—and often it isn't!—gossip can still be harmful. At best, it's using someone else to feed our egos. At worst, it can ruin a person's life. And attempting to disguise gossip as Christian concern—"Here's a prayer concern"—doesn't help one bit.

Closely related to gossip is the sin of slander—making a false statement or misrepresentation that damages another person's reputation to gain an advantage over that person. Political campaigns are notorious for doing this, but Christians do it too. We slander when we ascribe wrong motives to people, accuse our fellow Christians of not being godly enough, misrepresent another person's views without first determining what those views are, or blow other people's failings out of proportion.

Slander is actually a form of lying, but it's not the only one. Most of us will avoid making a blatantly false statement, but exaggeration, failing to tell the whole truth, or indulging in "little white lies" also count as "corrupting." So does critical speech—negative but unnecessary observations such as "That shirt looks awful on him!" or "She just can't sing."

Sins of the tongue can involve the way we talk *to* one another as well as the way we talk *about* one another. "Talking to" sins include harsh words, sarcasm, insults, and ridicule, usually driven by impatience or anger and intended to put down, humiliate, or hurt others.

Ephesians 4:29 says all these forms of "corrupting talk" need to be replaced with words that build up others and give grace. So we need to ask ourselves some questions before we speak: *Will what I'm about to say tend to tear down or build up the person I want to talk about? Is it true? Is it kind? Does it need to be said?*

Jesus said, "Out of the abundance of the heart the mouth speaks" (Matthew 12:34). This means that although we speak of sins of the tongue, our real problem is our heart. The tongue is only the instrument that reveals what's really in our hearts.

For some years I have sought to apply Ephesians 4:29 to my speech. I'm sure I fail many times, but at least that's the target I aim for. One night I started to say something negative to my wife about a former colleague but held my tongue. And I was feeling pretty good about my self-control until something occurred to me: "But you thought it, didn't you?" I realized I needed to guard not only my mouth, but my heart as well.

David prayed, "Let the words of my mouth and the meditation of my heart be acceptable in your sight, O LORD, my rock and my redeemer" (Psalm 19:14). I have learned to pray this also. I still use Ephesians 4:29 as a guideline, but now I try to apply it to my thoughts as well as my speech. I'd like to have no corrupting thoughts come out of my heart but only thoughts that, if uttered, would build up those who hear them.

If you and I truly want to put on the new self created after the likeness of God in true righteousness and holiness, we must make Ephesians 4:29 one of our guiding principles. So take a few moments to reflect on this chapter and your own speech patterns. Do you spread rumors or put down others? Do you show impatience or anger through unkind words that humiliate or hurt? If you're not sure, ask your friends or your family. They'll know!

Remember, we're talking about real sin. The kind of speech we've discussed in this chapter may seem acceptable to us, but it is not acceptable to God. It truly is sin.

# YOUR TURN

"Let no corrupting talk come out of your mouths, but only such as is good for building up, as fits the occasion, that it may give grace to those who hear." (Ephesians 4:29)

## ENGAGE

1. "Any speech that tears down another person—someone we are talking about or someone we are talking to—is sinful speech." Do you agree or disagree with this statement? Why?

   *Yes, I whole-heartedly agree because any speech that tears down is hurtful + sinful → it seeks to hurt + wound the person*

2. How do you think humor fits into this issue of corrupting speech? Where's the line between edgy humor and corrupting speech?

   *humor → stupid talk edgy humor?*

3. If you decided to take Ephesians 4:29 seriously, what changes would you need to make in your life? Which of these do you think would be most difficult? *I'd have to start with my heart, but I struggle with critical speech, gossip, and sarcasm → All of them*

## BRING IT TO GOD

Pray out loud David's prayer from Psalm 19:14: "Let the words of my mouth and the meditation of my heart be acceptable in your sight, O LORD, my rock and my redeemer."

# CHAPTER 20

# WORLDLY

"Do not love the world or the things in the world," wrote the apostle John (1 John 2:15). Those who do that are called worldly. It's kind of an old-fashioned word. And Christians don't always agree about what is worldly and what isn't.

For our Amish friends, *worldly* refers to such conveniences as electricity, telephones, and automobiles. For the very conservative church where I grew up, *worldly* applied to a list of prohibited activities such as dancing, card playing, and going to movies. But the problem of worldliness is actually much broader than a list of prohibited activities or modern conveniences.

A passage in 1 Corinthians can help us understand the more "acceptable" aspects of worldliness and how it relates to our subtle sins. Paul urged the Corinthians to "use the things of the world, as if not engrossed in them. For this world in its present form is passing away" (7:31, NIV). In other words, we should handle even the legitimate things of the world with care lest they become too important to us.

Based on this explanation, I define worldliness as *being attached to or preoccupied with the things of this temporal life*. What we're attached to may or may not be sinful in itself, but the high value we put upon it makes us worldly.

"Set your minds on things that are above," Paul urged, "not on things that are on earth" (Colossians 3:2). Our focus and priority should be spiritual, our highest value placed on God-related pursuits: Scripture, prayer, the gospel, obedience to God, the fulfillment of the Great Commission, and eternal life, not to mention God Himself.

The non-Christian world clearly does not focus on these things. Most of our nice, decent, but unbelieving friends are only interested in the world around them. Yet their lifestyles are usually not so different from ours. They go to class, hang out, text their friends, try not to get in trouble—just like we do. That's why living among them makes worldliness feel so acceptable to us. So we can further develop our understanding of worldliness by this secondary definition: *Worldliness means accepting the values, attitudes, and practices of the nice but unbelieving society around us without discerning whether or not those values, attitudes, and practices are biblical. Worldliness is just going along with the culture around us as long as that culture is not obviously sinful.*

Worldliness is a broad subject worthy of an entire book, and I'm devoting only a chapter to it. So I'm going to limit our discussion of it to three areas I believe have become acceptable sins to many of us: money, immorality, and idolatry.

But aren't immorality and idolatry obviously unacceptable to Christians? Not always! We'll be looking at certain aspects of both that have become familiar and acceptable to many Christians. As for money, which can also involve obvious sin (such as stealing it!), we'll also limit ourselves to what seems generally acceptable to most people.

## MONEY

What we do with our money tells us a lot about what we care about, and it can be a sad tale.

In 2004, for example, the average household income after taxes was $52,287. As I mentioned in chapter 13, the average household credit-card debt was $7,000. But the average household's giving for all causes was a mere $794—about 1.5 percent.[1]

These statistics are, of course, based on our entire population. Evangelicals do better than that, but not by much. In a 2003 survey, members of eight evangelical denominations gave 4.4 percent of their income to God's work. This was actually a decline from the 6.2 percent that members of those same denominations gave in 1968.[2] If those eight denominations reflect evangelicalism as a whole, evangelicals are becoming less generous toward God with their money—and more like society in general.

If our giving is decreasing and our debt is increasing, what are we doing with our money? Certainly not saving it—our average savings is only 2 percent of our income. What we're doing is spending—buying such things as houses, cars, clothes, vacations, and electronics. We have become worldly in our use of money.

How much *should* we be giving? The Old Testament standard was the tithe—10 percent of income. A person who makes $10,000 gives $1,000. Someone who makes $100,000 gives $10,000. The kid who makes $50 in babysitting money gives $5.

As we've seen, average giving among evangelicals is less than half of that.

There is some disagreement about whether the tithe applies to Christians, although the concept of *proportionate giving*—giving "according to what a person has" (2 Corinthians 8:12)—is clear in the New Testament. But I don't believe this disagreement is the reason tithing has fallen on hard times. The reason is worldliness. When it comes to money, we're focused on the things of earth, not the things of God.

Jesus said, "You cannot serve God and money" (Matthew 6:24). But in the lives of many Christians, money is winning. And the Bible clearly says, "The love of money is a root of all kinds of evils. It is through this craving that some have wandered away from the faith and pierced themselves with many pangs" (1 Timothy 6:10).

If money wins out in our lives, God's not the one who loses. He doesn't need our money. But if we spend all our money on ourselves, we're the ones who become spiritual paupers.

But what if someone cannot afford to give 10 percent? That's between the person and God. As 2 Corinthians 9:7 puts it, "Each one must give as he has decided in his heart, not reluctantly or under compulsion." But can I tell you my story?

Years ago, when I left industry to become a staff trainee with The Navigators, I took a 75 percent cut in salary. I was financially shell-shocked. "I can't afford to tithe," I thought. "Surely God accepts my really low income doing His work as my giving." But my conscience kept bugging me, so I finally decided I would tithe my meager income and trust God to provide.

About that time I was drawn to the story of Elijah being fed by the widow of Zarephath (see 1 Kings 17:8-16). She was down to the last bit of food in her house, expecting to prepare a last meal for her son and herself and then die. Yet Elijah said to her (I'm paraphrasing), "Feed me first, for God will provide for you." The widow did as Elijah instructed her, and God did provide. The Bible says, "The jar of flour was not spent, neither did the jug of oil become empty, according to the word of the LORD that he spoke by Elijah" (verse 16). I began to pray over that verse, and I can tell you that throughout fifty-two years of ministry and tithing, God has always provided.

We need to remember that, as we saw in chapter 10, everything we have and our ability to earn more comes from God. Giving back 10 percent of what He has given us is a tangible expression of our recognition of that and our thanksgiving to Him for it.

Finally, we need to remember the infinite generosity of our Lord in giving Himself for our salvation. As Paul wrote the Corinthians, he said, "You know the grace of our Lord Jesus Christ, that though he was rich, yet for your sake he became poor, so that you by his poverty might become rich" (2 Corinthians 8:9). Our giving should reflect the value we place on His gift to us.

## VICARIOUS IMMORALITY

You are no doubt wondering how immorality could ever be considered a respectable sin. Let me say right off that we are not going to address things like adultery or pornography here. Those actions are beyond the scope of this book, where we are looking at the sins that Christians tolerate.

So how do we tolerate immorality? We do it by what a friend calls vicarious immorality. *Vicarious* means "experienced indirectly." Someone else does something, but you enjoy that experience by watching or reading or some other means.

Do you enjoy reading blogs about celebrities who sleep around and trash motel rooms and otherwise act badly? That's vicarious immorality.

Are you hooked on television shows where people lie and cheat and treat each other viciously? That's vicarious immorality.

Do you go to movies or watch television programs knowing that sexually explicit sins will be shown or read novels knowing that such scenes will be described? That's vicarious immorality.

It's clear the world around us enjoys this sort of thing. After all, those tabloids and reality shows and movies and novels wouldn't be produced if people weren't buying them. This is one instance of values and practices accepted by society around us that are clearly contrary to Scripture. And to the extent that we follow along, we are worldly.

Then there is the area of fashion. The specifics change, but immodest dress in some form — too short, too tight, too much cleavage, underwear showing, no underwear at all — has been a fashion staple for decades now. As I walk along airport concourses or in shopping malls where large crowds of people gather, I'm constantly having to turn my eyes away from looking at something I should not see. Male students tell me this is a big problem on their high school and college campuses.

So there are two areas under this subject in which Christians can become worldly. First, many Christian women seem more concerned about what is fashionable than they are with what is biblical. According to 1 Timothy 2:9, Christian women are to dress with modesty and self-control. If you simply go along with the immodest fashions of the day, you are worldly in this area of your life.

For the men, our problem is looking. I'm not just talking about looking and then entertaining sexual fantasies. Even to linger with eyes and enjoy what women expose or accentuate by what they wear is sin. Yes, we are only doing what otherwise nice, decent men around us are doing. But in that sense, we are worldly.

A younger man recently asked me how I handle this temptation. I told him my first line of defense is Proverbs 27:20, which I learned in the King James Version many years ago: "Hell and destruction are never full; so the eyes of man are never satisfied." The application to me is that one lingering look never satisfies; it just whets the appetite for more. So don't linger over what you should not be looking at. Look away!

My second line of defense is Romans 6:21: "What fruit were you getting at that time from the things of which you are now ashamed? For the end of those things is death." I ask myself what fruit or benefit I receive from indulging in a lustful look. Only the fleeting pleasures of sin, followed by thoughts of shame and regret. So guys, let's commit ourselves to dealing with this area of worldliness.

# IDOLATRY

As we come to this section of worldliness, we again need some explanation. Obviously we are not worshipping idols of wood, metal, and stone these days. Our problem is what some call "idols of the heart." In this sense, an idol can be anything we place such a high value on that it tends to absorb our emotional and mental energy, or our time and resources. Or it can be anything that takes precedence over our relationship with God.

An object such as a car or a really great phone can be an idol. So can an activity (shopping and gaming) or a status (being popular or cool). I've seen lots of instances where a person's career or vocation becomes an idol. The person becomes so obsessed with getting ahead that God takes second place. And for some Christians, political and cultural issues take on idol status. While I believe it is important for Christians to be knowledgeable and even involved in important issues, we have to be careful that we don't make idols of our political parties or our cultural concerns.

A very common example of modern-day idolatry is our consuming passion for sports. I know I may be stepping on some toes here. But I don't think there's any doubt that sports have become idols in our culture. High school and college football is often spoken of as a religion in many states, and many coaches make huge salaries. Parents spend large portions of their lives ferrying kids to soccer games, swim meets, and cheer competitions. And church services are often let out early to make sure members don't miss a kick off.

I'm a graduate of a school whose football team has been a major powerhouse over the years. They've won seven national championships, the first of which occurred when I was a junior. I give you this background to explain why my school's football fortunes became something of an idol to me. Even years after I graduated, I would grow tense on Saturday game days, as if my happiness depended on the game's outcome.

I'm still a fan of my university's football team, and I'm pleased when they win. But it's no longer an idol for me. God convicted me of my idolatry, and I now remind myself that football is only a game. A win isn't a way to glorify God; if anything, winning just panders to our pride. And getting too caught up in sports is just another form of worldliness.

That brings us back to the twofold definition of worldliness. Worldliness, remember, is a preoccupation with the things of this earthly life. It's also accepting and going along with the values and practices of our society without discerning if they are biblical.

Those two words *going along* are key. We just do it without thinking. That's why most Christian young women dress immodestly. They're simply going along with what others are wearing without stopping to think whether or not those styles are pleasing to God. And there is nothing overtly sinful in sports themselves. But if we simply go with the flow, we can end up making an idol of our favorite team.

So how can we deal with our worldly tendencies? It's always a good idea to actually stop and think about what we're doing! But instead of trying to become less worldly, why not focus on becoming more godly? The more we grow in our relationship with Him, the more we will view all aspects of our lives through the lens of His glory, and it's amazing how our view of the world around us will change.

# YOUR TURN

"Use the things of the world, as if not engrossed in them. For this world in its present form is passing away." (1 Corinthians 7:31, NIV)

## ENGAGE

1. Although the Bible clearly tells us not to "love the world or the things of the world," Christians often disagree on the specifics. What one person thinks of as harmless, another calls worldly and sinful. So how do we decide where to draw the line? Do you agree with the examples in this story? *Get in God's word.*
   *Yes*

2. "By the count of most scholars, Jesus speaks more often about money than any other topic (almost 2 to 1). [He] speaks more often about money than he does about sin, salvation, prayer, sex . . . anything."[3] Why do you think He did this? *Once you have money, you can almost do anything*

3. What would you say are the three biggest idols among people your age? How do we know if something's become an idol for us? How do we break free? *Entertainment, friends, Sports. If it's all we think about — Put God 1st*

4. This chapter says, "Instead of trying to become less worldly, why not focus on becoming more godly?" What are some practical strategies for doing that? *Love His word, Love God, Be thankful*

## BRING IT TO GOD

Write down three ways you believe you've been "going along" with the culture instead of asking yourself what is biblical and godly. Confess these to God and ask Him to bring you closer to His heart.

# CHAPTER 21

# WHERE DO WE GO FROM HERE?

We've now looked in detail at the subtle or sneaky sins we Christians tolerate in our lives. And to tell the truth, I hope this journey has been at least a little painful for you. That means you have been honest enough and humble enough to admit some of your own subtle sin. That's a good thing, a hopeful thing, because "God opposes the proud but gives grace to the humble" (1 Peter 5:5).

Jesus said basically the same thing in the part of His Sermon on the Mount usually called the Beatitudes (see Matthew 5:1-12). He started by talking about the "poor in spirit" and "those who mourn"—in other words, those who are conscious of their own sinfulness. Because of this, they are "meek" and "merciful" in their attitudes and actions toward others, and they "hunger and thirst for [the] righteousness" they know they haven't attained yet. They're the opposite of proud, morally superior, and self-righteous! And Jesus said that they are "blessed"—happy!

A lot of Jesus' parables make more or less the same point. Consider the parable of the Pharisee and the tax collector praying in the temple (see Luke 18:9-14). To the Jews who first heard this story, the tax collector would have been the automatic bad guy. Everybody hated tax collectors. And in the parable of the prodigal son (see Luke 15:11-32), the son's despicable actions—taking his father's money, wasting it all on immoral living, sleeping with unclean pigs—would have completely scandalized Jesus' Jewish audience. That son would have been a bad guy too.

But read those stories again. The real bad guys are the self-righteousness Pharisee and the self-righteous older brother! The humble, repentant tax collector went away justified, and the repentant prodigal son got a big hug of welcome from his father. Doesn't this tell us something about how much God responds to a humble and contrite spirit?

We need to be honest and humble enough to admit our subtle sins in order to experience the love that comes through the forgiveness of those sins. But we must also face them in order to deal with them. The worst sin of all, in practical terms, is the denial of the subtle sins in our lives. We cannot fight them until we admit their presence. The first step in breaking free from any sin is to acknowledge it and repent of it.

This doesn't mean we will make rapid progress in getting that sin out of our lives! The flesh doesn't give up that easily. Besides, most of us have developed patterns of sinning. We have developed habits of ungodly thinking, anxiety, self-indulgence, critical attitudes, gossip, and the like. So even though you've finished this book, you probably have some work to do.

So what's next? I hope that you've been praying over these so-called respectable sins all along, asking God to reveal to you any evidence of them in your life. But this is a good time to look at the list again. Turn back to the survey you took before you started looking at these sins in detail. As you go through it, continue to ask God to open your eyes to sins you have been tolerating or have even refused to acknowledge as being present in your life.

This might be a good time to ask others for their evaluation too. Set aside time with someone who knows you well: a good friend, a brother or sister, a youth leader, even your parents. Ask for honest feedback, and try not to get defensive when you get it. Just listen, even if you don't agree with their assessments. God may be using other people to open up areas you have been in denial about.

Now go back and review the seven general directions for dealing with sin listed in chapter 6. If you are feeling a little overwhelmed about all this, pay special attention to number 1: always address your sin in the context of the gospel.

Remind yourself that your sins are already forgiven, your guilt is taken care of, and the Holy Spirit is acting in your life to free you from the power of sin. As you work on your sins, you're growing into those qualities Paul called the fruit of the Spirit: "love, joy, peace, patience, kindness, goodness, faithfulness, gentleness, self-control." Best of all, you're becoming who you already are—a saint!

Don't make the mistake of thinking that sneaky "little" sins don't matter. The world is watching us, and they notice our self-righteousness, our anger, our judgmentalism, and especially our hypocrisy. They know when we don't practice what we preach. But the more we respond in honesty and humility, the better our chance of changing their minds while we're changing our lives. We might even win some hearts for God even as we draw closer to the One who loved us enough to die for our sins.

# YOUR TURN

"The fruit of the Spirit is love, joy, peace, patience, kindness, good-ness, faithfulness, gentleness, self-control; against such things there is no law." (Galatians 5:22-23)

## ENGAGE

1. Think back on your study of this book. Identify three key discoveries or principles that stood out to you regarding God's view of the "respectable sins," our tendency to overlook these sins, or God's provision for overcoming them. What comes to mind?

*Discontentment, jealousy
Idolatry*

2. Look over the prayer you wrote at the end of chapter 5. Have you made progress in dealing with this sin or any of the subtle sins you've identified? Have you run into any roadblocks?

3. Name at least one strategy for dealing with subtle sin you would like to continue after this study is over.

*→ Scripture memory*

## BRING IT TO GOD

What would you like to tell or ask God right now regarding "respectable sins" in your life? Write out your prayer as if He's reading over your shoulder. Don't forget to express your thanks for bringing you this far and for your dependence and trust in Him to help lead the godly life He desires for you.

# A GUIDE FOR GROUP LEADERS

*espectable Sins Student Edition* makes a rewarding group study for students. This brief guide is intended to help you lead your group through an enriching time of discovery.

You'll probably want to combine chapters to get through the book in a reasonable period of time. The following plan will take you through the book in nine weeks. Feel free to adapt this plan to cover a longer or shorter period of time.

- Week 1: Introduction and chapters 1–3
- Week 2: Chapters 4–6
- Week 3: Chapters 7–8
- Week 4: Chapters 9–10
- Week 5: Chapters 11–12
- Week 6: Chapters 13–14
- Week 7: Chapters 15–16
- Week 8: Chapters 17–18
- Week 9: Chapters 19–21

Be sure each participant has his or her own copy of the book. And it goes without saying that you should be thoroughly familiar with the material before each group session. Note the "Your Turn" section at the end of each chapter that includes a Scripture for participants to read or memorize, questions to help them engage with the material, and a prayer prompt. If you are following the plan above, you will have 6–12 discussion questions to choose from, but you are invited to craft your own as well. Be sure to pray for God's wisdom, guidance, and sensitivity as you prepare and facilitate. Pray for His profound work in the heart and life of each participant.

The survey/self-test "Are You a Respectable Sinner?" can be a helpful tool for you at several different points of your study. It's a fun way to introduce the study and a helpful wrap-up as well, or you can use it at both beginning and end to highlight participants' growth through the study. The survey also works well in conjunction with "The Directions" in chapter 6.

Be sensitive about how much you ask the students to share about their survey responses. If you sense they might be uneasy about revealing their personal failings, encourage them to fill in the survey privately, between sessions, or to answer it according to what they've observed in their churches or youth groups. (You'll find that young people have a keen nose for hypocrisy!)

Encourage participants to read the assigned chapters before each meeting and, if possible, to work through the "Your Turn" sections on their own before sessions. Remind them that it's okay to write in their books or write down their responses and prayers in a separate notebook.

Start each group session by encouraging participants to share their general response to the reading and their personal discoveries, then use the "Engage" questions to stimulate discussion. For some questions you might pose the question to no one in particular and wait for responses. As much as time permits, encourage unrushed, multiple responses. Here too, allowing students to talk about what they've observed as well as what they've done can reduce the pressure on them.

Be sure to conclude your sessions by praying together. The "Bring It to God" prompts give you a place to start, but feel free to vary your approach depending on the direction the session has taken. You can have one person pray or open the session up for brief conversational prayers from anyone who wishes to pray aloud, but make sure no one feels pressured or obligated.

May God richly bless you and your group as you read and discover His blessings together.

# NOTES

## CHAPTER 2: ME — A SINNER?

1. Peter Barnes, "What! Me? A Sinner?" *The Banner of Truth*, April 2004, 21.
2. Karl Menninger, *Whatever Became of Sin?* (New York: Hawthorne, 1973), 14–15.
3. Barnes.

## CHAPTER 3: SPIRITUAL CANCER

1. Ralph Venning, *The Sinfulness of Sin* (Carlisle, PA: Banner of Truth Trust, 1965; first published 1669), 31.

## CHAPTER 4: THE GUILT CURE

1. Brian H. Edwards, *Through Many Dangers: The Story of John Newton* (Welwyn, England: Eurobooks, 1980), 191.
2. An alternate reading of the last phrase is "Save from wrath and make me pure." Of ten hymnals I consulted, five use the phrase I have used. Five use the alternate reading. Either way, the meaning is ultimately the same.
3. An exposition and application to life of some of these Scriptures is included in chapter 6 of my book *The Gospel for Real Life,* also published by NavPress.

## CHAPTER 8: ANXIOUS AND FRUSTRATED

1. I am aware that some people suffer from extreme anxiety attacks that are totally consuming and often result in physical complications. These cases may require professional help and are beyond the scope of this book. I am dealing with what we might call the anxieties of ordinary, daily life.

## CHAPTER 9: DISCONTENT

1. I have dealt with these attributes of God more in depth in my book *Trusting God: Even When Life Hurts* (NavPress).

## CHAPTER 11: PROUD

1. The term "humblebrag" was coined by screenwriter Harris Wittels, who collected these kinds of statements on his Twitter feed and then in his book *Humblebrag: The Art of False Modesty* (New York: Grand Central Publishing, 2012).

## CHAPTER 14: IMPATIENT AND IRRITABLE

1. This expression is taken from the title of Paul David Tripp's book *War of Words* (Phillipsburg, NJ: P&R, 2000). I highly recommend this excellent book.

## CHAPTER 15: ANGRY

1. Robert D. Jones, *Uprooting Anger* (Phillipsburg, NJ: P&R, 2005), 13.
2. I am indebted to Robert Jones for these thoughts, though I have not quoted him exactly. For readers who want to pursue the subject of anger beyond this chapter, Jones's book *Uprooting Anger* is an excellent resource.
3. Again I know that I have treated this subject lightly. Jones has an excellent chapter in *Uprooting Anger* that deals extensively with the subject of anger against God.

## CHAPTER 16: IN THE WEEDS

1. Some readers may wonder why I do not refer to the phrase "root of bitterness" in Hebrews 12:15 as a warning against the sin of bitterness. The expression is an allusion to Deuteronomy 29:18 and the phrase "poisonous and bitter fruit," which in that passage speaks of inward, heart rebellion against God. In Hebrews 12:15, the writer was using that expression from Deuteronomy to warn against apostasy, not the bitterness of ongoing resentment.

## CHAPTER 20: WORLDLY

1. Joel Belz, "Stingy Givers," *World Magazine*, June 24, 2006, 4.
2. Belz, 4.
3. Curtis Chang, "What the Bible Says About Money: Investing in the Kingdom" (lecture notes, Urbana '96 Student Missions Conference, University of Illinois at Champaign-Urbana, IL, December 1996), http://www.intervarsity.org/mx/item/4720/download/.

# ABOUT THE AUTHOR

JERRY BRIDGES is an author and Bible teacher. His most popular book, *The Pursuit of Holiness*, has sold over one million copies. He is also the author of *Trusting God*, *The Discipline of Grace*, *The Practice of Godliness*, *The Fruitful Life*, *The Gospel for Real Life*, and *The Transforming Power of the Gospel*. Jerry has been a full-time staff member with The Navigators for many years and currently serves in the collegiate ministry.

# Go through the book alongside your teen.

**Respectable Sins**
Jerry Bridges

All sins are considered equal in God's eyes, but it seems we have created a sliding scale where gossip, jealousy, and selfishness comfortably exist within the church. Acclaimed author Jerry Bridges believes that just as culture has lost the concept of sin, the church faces the same danger. Drawing from scriptural truth, he sheds light on subtle behaviors that can derail our spiritual growth.

978-1-60006-140-0

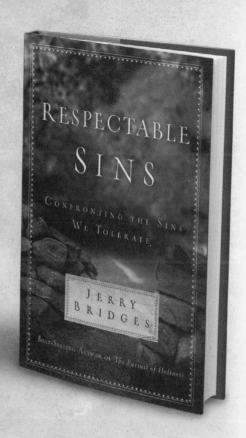

# MY LIFE IS **TOUGHER** THAN **MOST PEOPLE REALIZE.**

I TRY TO
KEEP EVERYTHING
IN BALANCE:
FRIENDS, FAMILY, WORK,
SCHOOL, AND GOD.

IT'S NOT EASY.

I KNOW WHAT MY
PARENTS BELIEVE AND
WHAT MY PASTOR SAYS.

BUT IT'S NOT
ABOUT THEM.
IT'S ABOUT ME...

ISN'T IT TIME I
OWN MY FAITH?

THROUGH THICK AND THIN, KEEP YOUR HEARTS AT ATTENTION, IN
ADORATION BEFORE CHRIST, YOUR MASTER. BE READY TO SPEAK
UP AND TELL ANYONE WHO ASKS WHY YOU'RE LIVING THE WAY
YOU ARE, AND ALWAYS WITH THE UTMOST COURTESY. 1 PETER 3:15 (MSG)

www.navpress.com | 1-800-366-7788     TH1NK by NAVPRESS

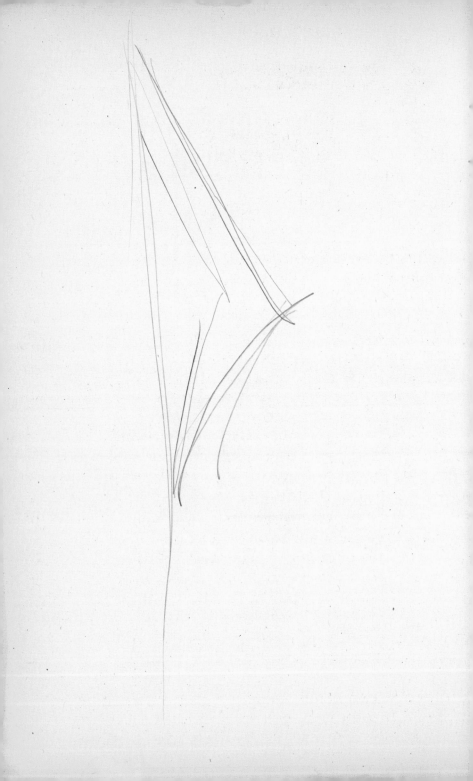